STUG III

Sturmgeschütz III
Ausführung A to G (SdKfz 142)

COVER IMAGE: **Sturmgeschütz III Ausf G.**
(Mark Rolfe)

First published in December 2019
Reprinted April 2021 and July 2022

A catalogue record for this book is available from the British Library.

ISBN 978 1 78521 213 0

Library of Congress control no. 2019943106

Published by J H Haynes & Co. Ltd.,
Sparkford, Yeovil,
Somerset BA22 7JJ, UK.
Tel: 01963 440635
Int. tel: +44 1963 440635
Website: www.haynes.com

Haynes North America Inc.,
859 Lawrence Drive, Newbury Park,
California 91320, USA.

Printed in India.

Senior Commissioning Editor: Jonathan Falconer
Proof reader: Penny Housden
Indexer: Peter Nicholson
Page design: James Robertson

STUG III

Sturmgeschütz III
Ausführung A to G (SdKfz 142)

Enthusiasts' Manual

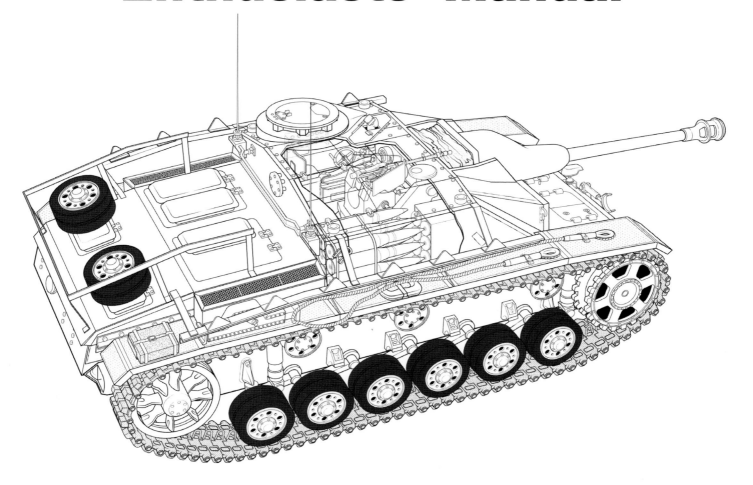

An insight into the development, manufacture and operation of the
Second World War German mobile assault gun and tank destroyer

Mark Healy

Contents

OPPOSITE An archetypal image of the problematic conditions experienced by the German columns advancing into Russia. Narrow earth tracks that passed for roads, flanked on either side by huge forested areas from which Russian infantry bypassed by the German armoured columns would emerge to attack follow-up supply columns. A number of the vehicles in the picture display prominent swastika flags to prevent attacks by the Luftwaffe.

Introduction

There is little doubt that the Sturmgeschütz III (StuG III) was one of the most important armoured fighting vehicles (AFVs) in the armoury of the German Wehrmacht in the Second World War. This is remarkable in that its origins were a matter of controversy and, had the tank supporters in the German Army had their way, it would have been stifled at birth. As it was it proved its mettle in the French Campaign of 1940, despite less than 30 being committed (the number was far fewer than had been anticipated, which was due to production delays and the ability of German industry to cater for the demand for military equipment across the board). Nonetheless, those few seem to have impressed and between the French surrender and the invasion of Russia just a year later, StuG formations

moved from being Batterien to Abteilungen. It was on the Ost Front that the StuG became far more than what perhaps it was intended to be. Up-gunned in 1942, it generated a formidable reputation as a tank destroyer and with the entry into production of the last model – the Ausf G in December 1942 – it was mass-produced for the first time. Serving on all fronts by the end of the conflict it was almost ubiquitous, the essential weapon needed to flesh out the panzers in the face of the ever growing Allied and Soviet tank fleets.

With the end of the war and the end of the StuG in production, the concept of a turretless AFV mounting a heavy gun seemed to die a death. Other than the Red Army no other power appeared to have faith in the notion. Nonetheless, it proved to be a formidable machine in its time.

BELOW A Sturmgeschütz Ausf C seen at the training ground for the Sturmartillerie at Jüterborg. Fifty of this model were built between May and September 1941.

Please note that this is a guide and as such the coverage of the assault gun can in no way be exhaustive. The presumption on the part of the author will be that having perhaps read this, one would want to go on and dig into the subject of the StuG in greater detail. There are some very fine books around that will permit you to do that. I list, what in my opinion are the best, in the bibliography.

Acknowledgements

Any book of this sort depends on the willing contribution of others to aid the effort. As ever my primary thanks goes to Thomas Anderson who has been so generous, once again, with his willingness to supply me with the bulk of the photographs of the StuG seen herein.

This is especially so as Thomas has his own books on the subject. Another individual may well have simply refused. My thanks also extends to his willingness to allow me to use some of the sources he uses in his books. While I am on the subject let me wholeheartedly recommend his two volumes on the StuG. As this title is far from exhaustive on the subject his volumes will provide any reader with an extremely comprehensive history of the employment of the StuG. It would also be remiss of me not also to extend my thanks to Herr Peter Müller of History Facts, who very kindly permitted me to use the graph on StuG production. I would also like to recommend History Facts' exhaustive and fantastically detailed coverage of the StuG that runs to three volumes.

In addition I wish to thank the archive section of the Tank Museum at Bovington in England, especially Katy. Also John St John Smith in the photography section who did such a good job producing the images for Chapter 6's walk-around of the museum's StuG III. Also Mark Rolfe, who beavered away so tirelessly to produce all of the three-view drawings of the different variants of the Sturmgeschütz III.

Last, but never least, is my wife Martha, who has always been so patient when I have been working, seemingly forever at this particular 'coal face', and to whom I give my grateful thanks.

Mark Healy, MA.
Dorset, August 2019

ABOVE A clear rear view of a Sturmgeschütz Ausf F/8 equipped with an L/48 75mm StuK40 main gun. This machine was built in 1942 and allocated to StuGAbt 232, surviving the winter fighting in Russia. In preparation for the 1943 summer campaign in southern Russia it was fitted with *Schürzen* (seen here) – the armoured skirts fitted to many German AFVs in the run-up to the Battle of Kursk, to give protection from the massed use of anti-tank rifles by Russian infantry. This Abteilung was fighting on the Mius Front.

Chapter One

From concept to eve of combat

The concept of the assault gun – a self-propelled, tracked, mobile artillery weapon for the infantry – first emerged in a document penned in 1936 by the future Field Marshal Erich von Manstein. The concept found sufficient support such that by the outbreak of war in 1939 the Sturmartillerie, as this new branch of the artillery had been designated, was established and set for expansion.

OPPOSITE Restored Sturmgeschütz III Ausf G from WTD 41 Trier. This vehicle (105251) was built in May 1944 by Alkett and served with the Finnish Army. *(Shutterstock)*

The renunciation of the restrictions of the Treaty of Versailles by Adolf Hitler in March 1935 and the passive acquiescence of Great Britain and France to the announcement had opened the way for a major expansion of the German Army beyond the 100,000-man limit imposed by the victorious Allied powers in 1919. Implicit in the German leader's public disavowal was also a rejection of those other clauses that had denied the Reichswehr access to the modern instruments of war now deemed so essential to the efficacy of any modern army – primarily that of tanks and heavy artillery. Indeed, included in his declaration was that the German Army would be expanded to 36 divisions. Then just a few months later the term Reichswehr passed into history when the Defence Law of 21 May saw the introduction of a new title, Wehrmacht, within which was created a Motorised Forces Command. By September this title was changed again, being transmuted into the more distinctive (and for the extremely vocal tank supporters within the Army the far more appropriate) title of the Armour Forces Command.

The late 1920s and early 1930s had seen a ferment of argument within the Reichswehr about the role of armoured forces in the future German Army. The advocacy on either side of the argument – that of the proponents of the creation of an independent armoured force and of those who opposed such a notion – was equally vehement. But by 1935 the debate had in principle been resolved in favour of the establishment of armoured divisions, but that did not of itself lead to the cessation of heated discussion about how such tanks were to be employed in the future German Army. Indeed, by the end of June 1935 the more detailed refinement of Hitler's demand for an army of 36 divisions had seen this translated by the senior German Army leadership into a plan for 33 infantry divisions and 3 armoured divisions. Aware as they were of Hitler's support for these new armoured formations, in October the newly created title of 'Inspectorate of the Armoured Forces Command' was given to Oswald Lutz, who was without doubt one of the seminal influences in favour of the armoured idea within the German Army. Heinz Guderian, who although just a colonel, was appointed to command the 2nd Panzer Division

at Würzburg, with the 1st, based at Weimar, under General Freiherr Maximilian von Weichs and the 3rd, at Berlin, was to be commanded by General Fessman. Despite his more lowly rank than that of the other two newly appointed divisional commanders, it was Guderian who was appointed Chief of Staff of the Armoured Forces Command. Thus began Guderian's rise as the foremost vocal (and for some, infamous) advocate of an independent tank arm.

In the short term there was the need for the provision of tanks for the fledgling panzer arm. Although 1935 had seen an increase in the number produced and delivered, they were of the Panzer I Ausf A that had entered service the previous year. The need for a better and more heavily armed tank had seen a contract issued in July 1935 for the Panzer II – a light panzer equipped with a 20mm cannon – with the first model of this heavier machine (7.9 tons) being trialled by the panzer divisions by the middle of the following year. Whereas the former was always envisaged as being a training tank and the latter a reconnaissance machine, the real core of the future Schnelltruppen – fast troops (this designation was employed until April 1943 when it was abandoned and replaced by the more widely embracing term Panzerwaffe) was to be vested in two larger and heavier machines. Guderian had strongly advocated the need for the development of two heavier and larger panzers that would provide the real core of the fighting power of the new armoured divisions.

The contract for the first of these and given the seemingly innocuous titles of 'medium tractor' or Zugführerwagen (platoon commander's vehicle) – being abbreviated to 'ZW' to disguise its true purpose – was issued at the tail end of 1934. Being a full-tracked machine and weighing in at some 15 tons, this was the tank that Guderian saw as being equipped with an armour-piercing main gun in a rotatable turret and envisioned becoming the mainstay of the panzer divisions. The second and heavier panzer was to weigh in at about 18 tons and was also given a title that disguised its true purpose, being designated as a Begleitwagen/'BW' – its true purpose being to provide firepower support to the 'ZW'. For that task, the 'BW' would necessarily require a bigger gun. Whereas the 'ZW' would come to be equipped with a 37mm KwK L/46.5 weapon, that of the 'BW' would be equipped with a 75mm KwK L/24 main gun. Initially known as the Geschütz-Panzerkampfwagen (75mm) (VsKfz 618), this was changed in 1935 to the more familiar designation Panzerkampfwagen IV (75mm) (VsKfz 622).

Given our concern with the origins of the Sturmgeschütz/assault gun, our focus resides with the early development of the 'ZW' or Panzerkampfwagen III, as it was to become better known. At the time of the initiation of the ZW project, its specification posed a major challenge to German industry, embracing as it did a raft of new technologies – hence the need to explore them via the creation of a 'development' series (Versuchserie) to test the various concepts and engineering solutions. The first of these series of ZW, was otherwise designated the Panzerkampfwagen III Ausf A (SdKfz 141). The ZW would run to three series before in December 1938 production began of the 4 serie ZW PzKpfw III Ausf E, which was the first model to go into regular production. However, the ZW designation would thereafter continue to be applied to all PzKpfw III models until the very last medium tank model – the Ausf L – was produced in 1942. Even so, by the time the first PzKpfw III Ausf A had entered service in 1937, the initial models of another vehicle utilising the Panzer III chassis and designed for the support specifically of the infantry had begun testing. Its existence certainly put the cat among the pigeons with Guderian and his coterie of panzer supporters who saw the emergence of this Sturmgeschütze as a primary threat to 'their' nascent tank arm.

The case for the Sturmartillerie

The notion of a tracked fire support vehicle for the infantry emerged from the fertile mind of Erich von Manstein who, on 1 July 1935, was appointed to the post of Chief of the Operations Branch of the Army General Staff. Just over a year later he was promoted once more to the rank of Generalmajor and became Oberquartiermeister I (Quartermaster General 1), thereby assuming the role of a Deputy Chief of Staff to Generaloberst Ludwig Beck, who

ABOVE Called the Father of the Sturmartillerie, Erich von Manstein penned the memorandum in 1936 to the head of the German Army that recommended the development of a specialised tracked armoured artillery vehicle to support the infantry. Herein lay the genesis of the assault gun, which was to emerge in the war years as one of the most significant armoured fighting vehicles of the Wehrmacht in the same fashion as von Manstein, promoted General-Feldmarschall in 1942, was recognised as possibly Germany's greatest soldier of the Second World War.

was serving as Army Chief of Staff. Although his First World War experience had been as an infantry officer, Manstein was no conservative, embracing with alacrity the post-war debate about the future direction of the Reichswehr and supporting the course advocated by the tank proponents. But Manstein recognised that the radical course they were set upon had also to embrace other arms of service including the infantry and artillery if its promise was to be realised. It was while Chief of the Operations Branch that von Manstein was to pen the memorandum that was to lead to the specification for a new type of infantry support vehicle – the assault gun. As such, Manstein was hoping to bring clarity to an ongoing debate between the infantry and artillery arms about the best way for the latter to support the former.

Notwithstanding the massive employment by the German Army of artillery in the First World War, it was recognised even then there were problems employing such in support of the more flexible and mobile operations of 1918. Although infiltration and speed were the essence of the tactics of these, infantry still found themselves in need of medium to heavy artillery support when objectives could not be so easily bypassed. Although an attempt had been made to equip infantry with light artillery by the provision of Begleitbatterien, this could not always be where needed when the speed of advance was dictated by the capacity of your horse teams to pull the guns across rutted and, in many cases, shell-hole-pocked terrain. Even if in theory it could have been, as the artillery was not under the control of the infantry, requests for its use had to be routed through the chain of command to headquarters – not a process designed to service the need for rapidity! Furthermore, in some cases, the speed of the infantry advance was so swift that they passed beyond the range of the artillery to provide fire-support when needed. Nor was it the case that the artillery could easily pack up their guns and equipment and follow up the advancing infantry in short order. Then were the problems of providing indirect artillery fire in that this presupposed the existence of observation posts, gun positions and depots able to supply ammunition and other matériel that permitted the guns to execute their task – none of which could be provided 'on the hoof'! Post-war, a partial redress to these problems was found in the provision of two artillery pieces to serve with the infantry and be under their control. The first – the 75mm le LG 18 had made its appearance in 1927, and the second, the much heavier 150mm SIG 33 – in 1933, the purpose of both being to provide the infantry with their own organic fire support. Nonetheless, they were still limited by virtue that they were either towed by horse teams or by wheeled transport. Although a partial solution, they did not address the need for a vehicle that could keep pace with the infantry, with such a notion pointing to the idea of a self-propelled weapon.

And it was to address this need in 1935 that von Manstein penned his memorandum both to the Chief of Staff and the Commander of

BELOW It was to von Fritsch, as Chief of the Army, that von Manstein's memorandum was directed. As an artillerist von Fritsch reacted in a very positive way to what was contained in the document, going so far as to want every infantry division to have a StuGBatterie of its own. Machinations by Himmler saw von Fritsch choosing to resign his job rather than be publicly impugned. The Sturmartillerie had lost an early and steadfast supporter.

the Army, General Werner Freiherr von Fritsch, outlining the concept of a self-propelled, tracked infantry support weapon that could:

'. . . accompany the infantry into the combat zone during the attack and breakthrough, and which would be in a position to immediately and effectively engage new targets as they appeared and put them out of action. This meant providing the infantry with an all-terrain, armoured weapon with heavy firepower . . . von Manstein made a proposition to reconsider some ideas with their roots in the use of an infantry escort weapon (Infanterie-Begleitbatterien) for First World War infantry. Taking advantage of possibilities offered by recent technical advances, he wanted to develop armoured cannon on self-propelled carriages for the direct support of the infantry.'

Manstein even gave a name to the concept in his memo – he called it the Sturmartillerie. A title designed to separate this from conventional artillery in order to ensure that it was perceived correctly: that is, that it was to be understood as an offensive weapon. Herein, then, lay the genesis of what was to be called the Sturmgeschütz or assault gun. As envisaged by him in his memorandum, each infantry division in the Army would be equipped with its own organic battalion of Sturmgeschützen comprising of 3 Batterien of 6 vehicles in each.

It should come as no surprise that the contents of Manstein's proposals drew down the ire of not only the tank supporters but also of the artillerists and anti-tank proponents, albeit for different reasons, each seeing in the proposals a threat to their own vested interests. Nor was this the only direction from which vocal criticism had been directed at the whole concept of the Panzerartillerie. Although we have alluded to the initial opposition to Manstein's proposals, this had become ever more vocal from many in the artillery arm itself. Indeed, the views expressed echoed many of the sentiments of those who earlier in the cavalry had argued against the idea of the introduction of the panzers.

'Even the Artillery Inspectorate initially resisted General von Manstein's ideas, and this resistance was reinforced by arguments from within its own ranks. The artillery resisted motorisation to a degree, which virtually reached pathological heights. The lack of appreciation, even detestation, of modern technology, and the advantages which it offered, initially went so far as to lead to serious proposals by the Artillery Inspectorate that the new support weapon be horse-drawn.'

His immediate superior, General Beck, himself an artilleryman, commented to Manstein that in this matter 'you have shot wide of the mark'. However, in the case of von Fritsch, the Commander of the Army, and also an artillerist, his ideas were received with greater sympathy. According to a recent biographer of von Manstein (see bibliography) he drew:

'. . . the commander-in-chief's attention to the fact that the artillery could now resume its historical role in taking direct part of the battle rather than just providing indirect fire. Apparently this appealed to the sense of honour of a former horse gunner and convinced Fritsch, as did Manstein's suggestion that the new weapon should be manned by the artillery rather than the infantry.'

Clearly Manstein knew his man, as Fritsch embraced Manstein's idea with alacrity and he sanctioned development of the new weapon. Indeed, his enthusiasm for the idea of the Sturmartillerie went further as it was Fritsch, who later in the autumn of 1937, sanctioned the plan to provide every active infantry division in the Army with a Sturmartillerie-Abteilung by the autumn of 1939, and with every reserve infantry division to possess one as well by the autumn of 1940, albeit with each battery reduced by 2 guns to 4. Even so, this plan was unrealistic in the light of the still limited tank output of German industry in 1937. Nonetheless, Manstein was sufficiently confident that the new weapon and the Sturmartillerie would now come to fruition, that in June 1936 he penned a follow-up to Fritsch in which he spelt out more clearly how this new branch of the artillery would operate. This was subsequently to set out the ground rules (doctrine) of the assault artillery and is provided in toto in the accompanying box. Although quite long it is deserving of careful scrutiny as it prefigures the manner in which the assault gun came to be employed with the coming of the war. This is as intrinsic to the development of the assault artillery as the technical details of its various variant iterations and their specifications.

The document was dated 8 June 1936.

Abt.Nr.890/36 g.kdos
To: The Chief of Staff of the Army

After the concept of the creation of armoured Sturmartillerie (assault artillery) met with the approval of the Chief of the General Staff, it seemed necessary to submit a tactical paper concerning the application of the assault artillery in addition to the technical development of the corresponding gun. Otherwise the situation will arise when we have the new weapon without knowing how to utilise it.

It can currently be said, not only with us but with other states as well, that the lines of thought about the utilisation of armoured vehicles and the assault gun are not clear-cut, and are many times quite blurred. On the one hand it is said that the armoured vehicle should take full advantage of its speed to break through enemy infantry in order to cripple the enemy Artillery and higher headquarters, and also to get to the enemy reserves. On the other hand it is said we cannot lose contact with the infantry, without which the very success of an armoured victory is in question. The armour branch is of the opinion that it is the job of the infantry to maintain contact, which means constant running for the infantry, and therefore an impossibility. The infantry wants to keep at least one wave of armour in their area, which in turn affects the speed of armour, and this is the very thing it uses for protection against enemy artillery.

Contrary to this it can be determined that although armour and assault artillery can be viewed as very similar weapons in a technical sense, they must be considered completely different branches in regards to tactics. No one in earlier times thought of attaching the infantry to the cavalry on the attack. And just as few people would have asked a cavalryman to attack in cadence with the infantry. It can therefore be easily concluded:

I. Armour units are combined arms units, whose composition makes it possible for them to fight independently to achieve their individual combat missions. If this quality is also to be applied to the armoured vehicle branch, then during the attack they will have motorised artillery for the exploitation of the success of the infantry, and moreover the necessary technical troops at their disposal.

    Tank units will be utilised in an independent role for strikes, most likely against the flanks and rear areas of the enemy, or at least on a fluid flank. They can also be given the mission of making a breakthrough of the enemy front. In any case, in order to attack independently they must have the necessary tools to fulfil the mission. As soon as one tries to couple them with other units, they lose the value of their nature.

    However, the possibilities for employing tank units is, as was in earlier times with the cavalry, considerably limited by terrain. Among other types, this includes forested areas, mountains, riverbeds and swamps which limit or rule out their utilisation.

    It will also be virtually impossible for them to achieve a breakthrough of a well-equipped enemy front. In such an instance, their effectiveness will be decisive if striking the enemy in a sensitive area and surprising him, in the case the enemy is not combat ready, or if they strike an already shattered enemy. To be utilised to the greatest advantage, they should be placed in a light Army (light Division, light Armoured Division, light Motorised Infantry Division).

II) Tank brigades, that is true armour brigades as one would better call them, are weapons of the main thrust of the attack. During the normal course of the attack, they should achieve a quick local victory within the framework of a corps or army. For this purpose, they should be coupled with an infantry division attacking in the main thrust, as opposed to tank units, which operate independently.

III) The Sturmartillerie (equally true if they are in the form of armoured vehicles or consist of armoured and motorised field guns) is, on the other hand, a weapon to assist the normal infantry division. Their use during the attack corresponds to the escort artillery of the last war. That is, the elite of the light artillery. In order to make them useful for other purposes, such as on the defensive, there is an additional requirement for the ability to be used as part of the normal artillery – in an indirect fire role, into the main battle area (usually a distance of 7km) at a minimum. Finally, they would be a superb offensive anti-tank weapon, and could replace the divisional anti-tank element in this role.

Assault artillery fights as escort artillery within the framework of the infantry. It does not attack like the tank, does not break through, but carries the attack of the infantry forward by quickly eliminating the most dangerous objectives through direct fire. It does not fight in large numbers like tank units, but is normally employed at platoon strength.

The platoon, or even the individual gun, makes a surprise appearance in and then quickly vanishes before it can become a target for the enemy artillery.

Being armoured and motorised permits the assault artillery to fight in among the infantry, which means the immediate combined effect at the right moment against decisive targets in a quantity which the artillery in rear positions is not able to deliver.

The gun must be able to take enemy machine gun emplacements out of action with a few rounds. It must also be able to knock out enemy tanks, in comparison to them it has inferior armour, but a superior ability to observe and shoot first.

Each infantry division should have at its disposal at least one battalion-sized unit of Sturmartillerie consisting of 3 Batterien of 6 guns each. One might even consider dropping either the normal artillery battalion or the divisional anti-tank battalion.

Above all, it can be seen that the Sturmartillerie should not be utilised in the sphere of armour units, but rather in that of a normal infantry division. A clean separation of the two branches is necessary if the two do not want to operate according to the improper doctrines.

The Sturmartillerie is to be trained as artillery units and will have to learn their mission as escort batteries in the environment of the infantry.

And finally in order to establish the tactical doctrinal basis, a battery from the Lehr-In.Btl. will be temporarily assigned to, and under the command of the Sturmartillerie for trial purposes in the interest of saving time. Initially, it should be sufficient for the battery to consist of six guns, on light tank chassis with temporarily mounted wooden guns, because the first order of business is the establishment and development of the tactics of the Sturmartillerie.

Signed,
Von Manstein.

The artillery embraces the Sturmartillerie

In fact, the speed with which the Army now grasped the nettle on the development of the Sturmartillerie was quite remarkable, given all of the other competing demands for resources of the growing German Army. The very first attempt to mount an artillery piece on a tank chassis so as to satisfy the assault gun concept for a turretless weapon was overseen by General Karl Becker, who was at the time Chief of Army Procurement and fully sympathetic to Manstein's ideas. He utilised an early Panzer II chassis but this was found to be inadequate. In the meantime, the 8th (Technical) Abteilung of the General Staff was commanded by another name – who, like Manstein, would become exceedingly well known in the second half of the coming conflict – was Walter Model. He was at the time an Oberst (Colonel) and was tasked with overseeing the development of the Sturmartillerie on behalf of the Heereswaffenamt. Within the 8th Abteilung the actual day-to-day responsibility for attending to this process was handled by Model's subordinate, Hauptmann Hans Röttinger. It was on 15 June 1936 that official sanction for the development of this new 'Begleitartillerie' – that is, the 'Armoured Artillery for Anti-Tank and Infantry' – was issued under the heading of document 449/36gKdos and from this would flow, in due course, the assault gun.
It set down the following requirements for the new machine with the first four requirements concerning its armament:

1) The new vehicle had to be equipped with a weapon of at least a 75mm calibre.
2) Although the superstructure was to be fixed on the chassis, the main gun was nonetheless to be able to traverse more than 30° without the vehicle having to turn on its tracks to facilitate this.
3) The gun had to be able to elevate to sufficient an angle to permit it to fire to a maximum of 6,000m.
4) The ammunition employed by the main armament must be able to penetrate all the types of armour known to be used at the time, at distances up to 500m.

The four remaining requirements were concerned with protection:

5) At this point in its development the assumption was that the new vehicle would be turretless and have an open top. The frontal armour would be angled at 60° and be sufficient to withstand fire from 20mm anti-tank rounds, whereas the side armour must be able to withstand small-arms armour-piercing rounds.

6) An essential requirement was that a complete machine stand no higher from the ground than a standing man to provide as small a target as possible.

7) Matters such as ammunition distribution, the number of crew and the type of communications equipment were to be finalised.

8) As of the time of the issue of 449/36gKdos no specific chassis had yet been identified on which to base this new machine.

The latter was, however, resolved when in 1937 it was determined that the chassis of the 'ZW' – the cover name for the Panzer III medium tank – would form the basis of the new Begleitartillerie.

The very first model of the PzKpfw III – the Ausf A – was built by Daimler-Benz and designated by them as Typ 1/Zug Führerwagen (ZW), 10 being built in 1936 with 3 being received by the 1st Panzer Division for testing before the end of that year. As was noted earlier, by virtue of the new technologies being created to service the original ZW specification, a series of development models were being produced and it was from the second of these that the first chassis on which to build the new machine were constructed. Twelve of these Typ 2/ZW Panzer III Ausf Bs were constructed by Daimler-Benz in 1937, with five of these being hived off to provide the basis for the five 'O' Serie of the Sturmgeschütz. Daimler-Benz was charged with the building of the first five of the 'O' Serie but by now it had come to be recognised that the Sturmgeschütz would need to be enclosed so as to protect the crew from air bursts. These five Versuchsgeräte (trial vehicles) would be constructed employing standard engineering steel for the superstructures and as such were never subsequently used in combat, although

they remained in service for some years after for training purposes. Krupp was contracted to adapt the 75mm L/24 gun – known as the s.Pak – which was already in service on the PzKpfw IV Ausf A, 35 of which they had produced by the end of 1937. As such, the performance of the weapon as fitted to the O Serie StuG and in all marks through to the Ausf E, was identical in performance and in ammunition types employed to that on the PzKpfw IV.

It was against this backdrop in the development of the Sturmartillerie programme that it received a setback flowing from machinations on the part of Heinrich Himmler to oust the head of the Army. Here is not the place to explore the activities of the Head of the SS and his assistant Reinhard Heydrich, but their motivations were scarcely disguised. Fritsch was an officer of the old school who believed in the separation of the military from politics, which is exactly the opposite of what Hitler wanted. He required a military imbued with the values and ethos of National Socialism and the Commander of the Army was instinctively opposed to this. Employing material that had come into his hands – but had to do with a lower ranking Army officer of the same surname, which was clearly known – nonetheless Himmler utilised the claim that Fritsch was a homosexual to prompt the general, who although vehemently denying the accusation, nonetheless felt his honour sufficiently impugned to choose to go into retirement on 4 February 1938. Having been hand-picked by Hitler, one of the first decisions of the more pliable Walter von Brauchitsch as Commander-in-Chief, had been to cancel his predecessors' order to expand the Sturmartillerie. This was obviously much to the delight of Guderian and his ilk as it would mean the Panzer III would be produced as purely a medium tank, with few numbers of its ZW chassis being diverted to service the building of the Sturmgeschütz. Nor was Manstein in a position to argue the case, as in the wake of Fritsch's departure he too was on the move, being posted away from Berlin as commander of the 18th Infantry Division at Leignitz. This was, however, but temporary, as he was recalled in very short order to higher duties as the Chief of Staff to General von Leeb

during the Munich Crisis in that same year. He therefore ceased to have any real input into the Sturmartillerie programme, although by 1938 it had acquired a life of its own.

It has been suggested that the decision by Brauchitsch to cancel the Sturmartillerie expansion order served to negatively impact on the StuG programme, but in truth, German industry was in no position in 1938 to service the demands of the growing panzer arm and also the Sturmartillerie. As it was, Daimler-Benz at the beginning of 1938 had started limited production of the fourth development model of the 3b Serie ZW/PzKpfw III Ausf D, of which just 30 were manufactured. The first actual model to enter extended production was the 4 Serie ZW/Panzer III Ausf F, the first of which did not leave the production line until December 1938. Ninety-six of this model were produced through to October 1939 with the manufacturing base widening from just Daimler-Benz to encompass the firms of Henschel and MAN. Even then this model evidenced teething problems, such that even by September 1939 and the invasion of Poland, a number of panzer divisions that had been scheduled to receive them had none

available for the campaign. As this variant was the basis of the adapted chassis selected for the production StuG III, it is hardly surprising that priority went to production of the Panzer III. This and other factors pertinent to the war situation at the end of 1939 and problems at Daimler-Benz accounts for why the very first production model of the StuG – the Ausf A – did not get produced until January 1940. But we are ahead of ourselves.

In the year between the issue of the specification for the Sturmgeschütz and the appearance of the first development machines in 1937, the antagonism directed towards the whole programme by Guderian and the 'tankists' had grown in volume and vehemence. They were uncompromisingly opposed to the whole idea, seeing the diversion of the still limited number of ZW chassis to servicing this programme as a dilution of the limited capacity of industry to build panzers. Even though it was pointed out to them that the assault gun, by virtue of lacking a turret was cheaper to produce, and would thereby permit a much more rapid growth in the number of armoured vehicles in the Army, this rationale was rejected by them out of hand.

ABOVE The formation of the 7./Artillerie-Lehr-Regiment (Mot) at the training ground at Jüterborg saw the beginnings of trials with the O Serie of StuG development machines.

For Guderian, the only armoured vehicle that mattered was one with a turret and he would maintain this antipathy to the turretless assault gun for years to come. Furthermore, that such a weapon would be operated by the artillery and not fall under the wing of the Panzertruppe further aggravated the matter. Indeed, the ire directed at all who supported the Sturmartillerie programme – and this included von Manstein, who by this date had been moved on from his position on the General Staff – bordered on the hysterical, being summed up by the claim that its proponents were, in fact, 'the grave diggers of the tank force'.

To Jüterborg

Nonetheless, it had been decided in late 1936 that the centre for this new artillery branch would be located at Jüterborg, which lies some 80km south-west of Berlin, with the training and development of operational procedures for the StuG made the responsibility of the 7th Batterie Artillerie-Lehr-Regiment – the Instructional Regiment of the Artillery (hereafter ALH). This was according to the guidelines laid down by the Artillery Inspectorate of the German Army High Command.

It now '. . . undertook the first field tests using wooden mockups, with good results. Even at this early stage it was evident that armoured support vehicles would be required for commanding and supplying the assault guns. The requisite orders were passed

BELOW Also known as the s.Pak, the 'O' Serie of StuGs were built on the chassis of Panzer III development machines. The image here shows an early StuG on fire while in the background is a Panzer III Ausf A sans its turret.

to the Heereswaffenamt and a large field manoeuvre was conducted in late 1937 at the Kummersdorff firing range.'

The outcome of which was very successful with those viewing the trial coming from 'a small, very critical circle from the German High Command, who were, however, convinced of its value'.

The first test battery was established the following year and in the spring of 1938 two available chassis equipped with dummy 75mm guns were available for development work. So as to preserve the secrecy of this project these vehicles were designated as 37mm Pak(sfl), which implied a much less powerful machine.

Even at this early stage the StuG development machines looked very similar to the service models, from Ausf A through to Ausf E, which would be produced between 1940 and 1942, apart from their employment of the Zw/PzKpfw III Ausf C and D chassis. The machine demonstrated at Kummersdorff was equipped with the 75mm KwK L/24 main gun, it carried 44 rounds of ammunition and was powered by a 300hp engine. Unlike the PzKpfw Ausf B, the StuG had 50mm frontal armour, not 30mm. The four-man crew assumed the positions within the hull and exercised the individual responsibilities that would characterise all StuG models through to 1945.

Throughout late 1938 and extending into early 1939 the small force of StuG IIIs employed at Jüterborg – comprising the five prototypes and a number of other PzKpfw III chassis that had been equipped with iron ballast to bring their weight up to that of the prototypes and equipped with dummy main guns – began intensive exercises with the Infanterie-Lehr-Regiment at Doberitz. These exercises served to translate theory into working practice such that insights and experience gained were incorporated into the doctrine that would underpin and guide the use of the Sturmgeschütz when finally they entered service, after production machines had begun to arrive and new units were formed.

One of the primary features that distinguished the manner of operation of Sturmgeschütz units from the outset was that being manned by artillerists – at this stage all of whom were volunteers – in contradistinction to that of the panzers, was the manner in which the former targeted and fired upon targets. Whereas gunners in tanks were trained to employ a method called 'walking their rounds' towards a target, which could involve employment of quite a few shells before hitting their target, the StuG gunner employed the well-attested artillery technique of bracketing a target to verify the range. This usually meant that the StuG would hit its designated target by the third shot almost 100% of the time. This

ABOVE Another O
Serie machine being
put through its paces
on the Jüterborg
driving range.

was certainly more economical on the use of expensive ammunition and it was some years into the war that the Panzertruppe (later the Panzerwaffe) adopted this method.

Setting up the first Sturmgeschütz-Batterien

It was intended to equip the first StuG unit in 1939, but a succession of delays did not see the initial production Ausf A leave Daimler-Benz's production line until January 1940, with the first of the machines arriving at Jüterborg later that month and being allocated to the very first Sturmgeschütz-Batterie, numbered 640. This had been established in November 1939 shortly after the conclusion of the Polish Campaign, with a further five Batterien being created through to July 1940. These were allocated the numbers 659, 660, 665, 666 and 667 and were located at two other centres in the vicinity of Jüterborg, at 'Dorf Zinna' and the 'Adolf Hitler Lager' sites. At the time it was planned that these Batterien would be established on the following dates:

- Sturmbatterie 640 1 November 1939
- Sturmbatterie 659 23 March 1940
- Sturmbatterie 660 23 March 1940
- Sturmbatterie 665 30 March 1940
- Sturmbatterie 666 30 March 1940
- Sturmbatterie 667 28 May 1940

As we shall see this timetable was over-optimistic in that Daimler-Benz, the contractor for building the assault guns, was slow in delivery of the necessary machines. By early 1940 this company had become overwhelmed by the sheer volume of work it had to address. Contracted to build the Panzer III, which had acquired priority in the light of the forthcoming campaign in the West, it also produced the 12-ton medium half-track prime mover, and the LG 3000 6 x 4 cross-country truck. In addition, Daimler-Benz found itself, along with Skoda, contracted to convert a large number of Panzer I Ausf B into Panzerjäger I equipped with a 47mm Czech-originated anti-tank gun in readiness for the Western Campaign. To this was added, after the conclusion of the Polish Campaign, damaged panzers and other vehicles returned from the East for rebuilding and rehabilitation. Such were the demands placed on Daimler Benz that the small productive capacity left over after these matters were addressed led to Sturmgeschütz production being necessarily delayed. Although this was only by a month, with the first StuG not being delivered as originally envisaged in December 1939, but January 1940. The upshot was this impacted on the scheduled delivery dates for all of the 29 other StuG IIIs Daimler-Benz was contracted to deliver, as was the case with the specialised support vehicles, which were also delayed. Indeed, it was only in the autumn of 1940, and after the conclusion of the French Campaign, that sufficient StuGs were produced for the first battalion, designated Sturmgeschütz Abteilung 184, to be formally established.

Sturmgeschütz-Batterie 640 was organised according to Kriegsstärkenweisung 445 (K.St.N.) (table of organisation), which was dated to 1 November 1939, with this document spelling out the numbers of StuGs and support vehicles each battery was to receive. In addition to the 6 Sturmgeschütz IIIs, each was to be equipped with 5 Leichte Gepanzerte Beobachtungskraftwagen SdKfz 253, a light half-tracked observation vehicle and 6 Leichte Gepanzerte Munitionskraftwagen SdKfz 252, half-tracked ammunition carriers, and three SdKfz 251/12 medium half-tracks. In addition, each Sturmbatterie was allocated

its own Werkstatt detachment comprising a single heavy 18-ton schwere Zugkraftwagen half-track and associated Sonderanghänger flat-bed to effect the recovery of damaged StuGs. There were, in addition, other assorted soft-skin vehicles for the transport of necessary fuel and supplies.

Preparing for 'Case Yellow' – the Campaign in the West

It had been Hitler's original intention to launch his offensive in the West even before the end of 1939. However, the weather and other factors such as the higher than expected losses and damage experienced by the Panzertruppe in the Polish Campaign and the need to rehabilitate that force prompted a whole series of cancellations leading to a major think about the execution of the offensive. When a launch date of early May 1940 was finally decided, part of the German Order of Battle for 'Case Yellow' would see the deployment and blooding in combat of the new Sturmartillerie.

Although, as we have seen, by November 1939 six Batterien had been established, the delay in the production of the machines to equip them was held up such that Sturmgeschütz-Batterie 640 – the very first to have been raised – did not begin to receive its

ABOVE The crew of a StuG Ausf A is awaiting ammunition supplies from the SdKfz 252 ammunition-supply half-track. On the left is the Sonderhänger 32 in which extra ammunition was carried.

planned vehicle allocation until February when the first four arrived at Jüterborg. Another 2 arrived the following month with just 13 having been received in toto by 1 May 1940. In consequence, even before the campaign in France began:

'. . . production delays of the StuG III Ausf A and its logistic vehicles were so severe that the first units deployed were lucky to see action in the Western Campaign. The first two completely equipped Sturmbatterien 640 and 659 were operational from the outset, Batterie 660 from 13 May 1940 and finally Batterie 665 by 10 June.'

Batterie 660, which it was intended would also be equipped, found its allocation of StuG Ausf As usurped by the decision to divert these to the Waffen SS. This was the first ever allocation of these machines – but certainly not the last – with OKH order KstN 90 establishing the first StuG Batterie to the Leibstandarte Adolf Hitler – this formation being the last to receive the Ausf A. In the meantime, the OKH had ordered on 16 May – six days after the beginning of the offensive in the West – that the date of the establishment of Sturmbatterie 666 was to be postponed, its actual date being contingent upon the availability of the

SDKFZ 252 AND SDKFZ 253

These two half-track vehicles were specifically designed to provide the necessary support for the assault gun formations, the need for which had been identified as early as 1937. The basis of both machines was the DEMAG-designed D7 tractor chassis on to which was grafted an armoured body designed to address the task each particular machine was designed to fulfil.

In the case of the Leichte Gepanzerte Munitionskraftwagen SdKfz 252, this was a light ammunition carrier that was employed to resupply the Sturmgeschützbatterien on the battlefield. It first left the production line three months after the first SdKfz 253. The 252 was easily identified by virtue of the very sharply angled rear section of its armoured body and was normally seen towing a Sonder Anhänger 3 1/1, which carried extra ammunition in addition to that carried in the 252. As of 1 November 1939, each Sturmbatterie was to be equipped with 6 x 252s with 2 serving with each of the 3 Zugs or platoons of the battery.

The 253 first went into production with Demag, with the first series of 30 being produced between June and August 1940.

ABOVE An SdKfz 252 and Sonderhänger 32 of the Infantry Regiment Grossdeutschland. In 1940 this was one of the few units to be equipped with these vehicles.

BELOW The SdKfz 253 Führerwagen was specially designed to function as a command vehicle for the Sturmbatterien. It was equipped with radios to permit the unit commander to effect command and control of the StuGs in his Batterie.

Production then shifted to Deutsche Werk before production of the type was terminated in September 1941 after a total of 413 had been produced. The role of ammunition resupply was thereafter undertaken by the SdKfz 250/6 leichte Munitionspanzerwagen Ausf A. This employed a standard 250 body adapted inside to carry ammunition for the StuG and it could carry 70 rounds within its hull. Unlike the 252, it did not have an armoured roof. It, too, employed a trailer on occasions to carry extra ammunition.

The need for an observation vehicle to serve alongside the Sturmgeschützbatterien had also been recognised as early as 1937, although it took until 1940 for the first of the specialised Leichte Gepanzerte Beobachtungskraftwagen SdKfz 253 or light armoured observation post to be produced. This machine, while using the same chassis as the aforementioned SdKfz 252, left the production line at Demag/Wegmann before the ammunition resupply variant, in March 1940. Sufficient had been produced by May 1940 and the beginning of the Campaign in the West for all four Sturmgeschützbatterien that participated to be equipped with 5 each – 1 serving with each of the 3 Zug (or platoons) and 2 with the Batterietrupp. It was the task of these to function as the command and control vehicles for the StuGs within their platoon. For this purpose they were equipped with both a radio transmitter and receiver – these being the FuG 15 and the FuG 16. In total, 285 were produced before production was terminated in June 1941, when the decision was taken to transfer the command function to a StuG in each platoon. To that end a number of StuG Ausf Ds were fitted with an extra pannier on the right side of the fighting compartment to take a transmitter so that a platoon commander could move forward with the other assault guns under his command. Nevertheless, in 1943, a leichte Beobachtungspanzerwagen or light observation post, again based on a SdKfz 250 chassis, was also provided. Allocated the designation 250/4, it was made available to assist the more numerous StuG battalions primarily operating on the Eastern Front. These vehicles also carried a FuG 15 and a FuG 16.

appropriate vehicles. This was followed just two days later with the order that 666 would now be established on 17 June with full combat readiness of the formation to be in place exactly a month later. The StuGs for the Batterie would be delivered by the end of June, this being enabled by Daimler-Benz being ordered to produce another six StuGs employing the 6/ZW hull of the PzKpfw III Ausf F/G.

When on 10 May the German offensive in the West opened, a maximum of just 24 Sturmgeschütz IIIs were committed to operations that lasted through to the end of June and the French surrender. The Sturmartillerie was blooded in this campaign from which the new weapon was to emerge with flying colours. The history of the StuG from May 1940 through to the end of the war in 1945 is addressed in Chapter 7 'StuG III in combat' found later in this text.

BELOW There were five SdKfz 253s to each Batterie. Two were with the Batterietrupp and one each Zug (platoon). Only 285 examples of this vehicle were produced. It was phased out in 1941 in favour of an adapted, normal-build SdKfz 250. Some examples survived until 1944.

Chapter Two

Short-barrelled StuG III Ausf A–E (SdKfz 142)

Entering delayed production at the beginning of 1940 and mounting the short-barrelled 75mm L/24 gun, the assault gun sporting this weapon would eventually run to five marks – A to E, before being replaced by the long-barrelled variant in early 1942. Apart from the Ausf A, which was produced by Daimler-Benz, the other variants B to E were produced solely by the Alkett company of Berlin.

OPPOSITE A short-barrelled StuG III of StuGAbt 192 raises the dust as it charges past horse-drawn transport at the beginning of Operation 'Barbarossa' in July 1941. Note the distinctive skull and crossbones unit insignia on the superstructure. *(Bundesarchiv)*

Our coverage of the production and marks of the Sturmgeschütz III is divided into two chapters. In this, the first chapter, are those that mounted the short-barrelled 75mm L/24 gun. That is Ausführung (Mk) A through to E. These were in production from January 1940 through to March 1942.

Thereafter all StuG IIIs produced were equipped with the long-barrelled 75mm L/43 or L/48 main gun or the 105mm StuH 42 L/28 howitzer. These were in production from March 1942 through to the end of the war. These are covered in Chapter 3, the second chapter.

All matters pertaining to the generic detailed nature of the StuG III internal hull, armour and armament design are addressed in Chapter 4 Anatomy of the StuG III.

Sturmgeschütz Ausf A (first series)

Built	Jan–May 1940
No built	30 (plus a further 6)
Fahrgestall Nummer	90001–900030 (first 30 Ausf A)
	90401–90406 (supplementary order)
Manufacturer	Daimler-Benz
Chassis employed	5/ZW (Pz IIIF)
Weight	19.6 tons
Engine	Maybach HL120

The contract for the construction of the first series of 30 Pz.Sfl.III (s.Pak), as the assault gun was still officially designated at the time,

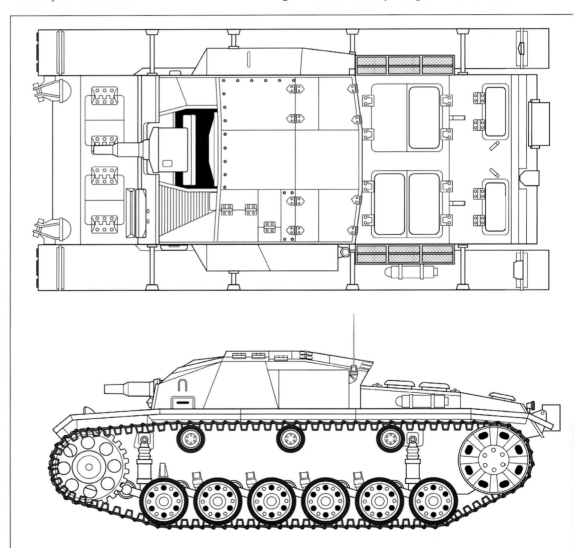

RIGHT StuG Ausf A.

(Mark Rolfe)

LEFT A StuG III Ausf A of Sturmbatterie 666 wearing both the narrower and wider road wheels, the former designed for the earlier 38cm-wide track and the latter for what was to become the standard 40cm track.

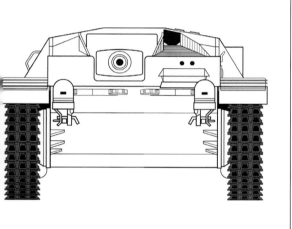

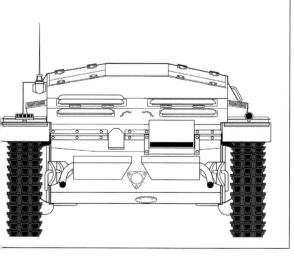

was awarded by the Heereswaffenamt to the Daimler-Benz company which, as we have seen, had designed the chassis of the new vehicle and its superstructure. That employed on the StuG Ausf A was based upon the 5/ZW chassis of the Panzer IIIF. The initial contract covered 30 Ausf As, this number being sufficient to equip five assault gun batteries.

These were to be assembled at the DB Werk 40 in Berlin-Marienfelde, which was also heavily engaged in the production of other types. Even though Daimler-Benz had managed to complete the first StuG chassis by December 1939, problems at the Krupp factory in producing the 75mm L/24 armament for the assault gun resulted in a slippage of the timetable by a month. In addition, the production of the StuG III was also impacted upon by the need of Daimler-Benz to attend to the damage incurred on Panzer IIIs that had taken part in the Polish Campaign. This made excessive demands on the spare parts inventory wherein those needed for the damaged Panzer IIIF (5/ZW) were prioritised at the expense of those same parts being required for the building of the StuG.

In consequence, the production of the first series of the StuG which, according to the memorandum of 14 October 1939, had been scheduled to begin in December 1939 and finish by 1 April 1940 so as to make way for the start of the production of the second series (that is the Ausf B, in that same month) was itself delayed.

ABOVE An example of the small series of StuG Ausf A2 that were made after the initial Ausf A was built by Daimler-Benz. As they were constructed directly on to a Panzer III chassis they retained some of the features of the tank, for example the brake ventilator hoods. These can be seen just inside the covers for the headlights.

Production of the first Pz.Sfl.III (s.Pak) now took place in January with the subsequent 29 having been manufactured by the end of May. The decision to create a sixth Sturmgeschützbatterie, not for the Army, but for the Waffen SS, saw Daimler-Benz receiving an additional contract to produce a further six StuG Ausf A. These employed the 6/ZW chassis of the Panzer IIIG and are distinguishable in that they mount armoured brake vents on the front of the hull.

This matter has caused no little consternation in terms of accounting of the numbers of Ausf A produced. However, Thomas Anderson, a recognised authority on the Sturmgeschütz III, has offered his own seemingly credible explanation to account for the anomaly. He suggests, that as per the original plan, six Sturmbatterien were to be the recipients of the 30 Ausf A but that Sturmbatterrie 666, which was due to be combat ready with its six machines by 20 June, saw its allocation diverted instead to the Waffen SS. These formed the SS Sturmbatterie of the Leibstandarte Adolf Hitler. In order to ensure that 666 received its machines it became necessary to utilise Panzer III Ausf F hulls to produce the Sturmgeschütz, these being allocated the chassis numbers 90401–90406.

Anderson observes that due to problems fixing the extra 20mm armour plate to the 30mm

of the front armour plate of the Sturmgeschütz that employed the Ausf F hull, these were in fact allocated to the Artillerie Lehr-Regiment at Jüterborg. In their stead Sturmbatterie 666 received six Ausf Bs, which were then allocated to Army Group North's Order of Battle for the forthcoming invasion of Russia.

For reasons that were not set forth in documentation, Alkett was contracted to produce an additional 20 StuG Ausf III Ausf A between June and September 1940. This short run was interpolated between the end of Daimler-Benz's contract for the first 30 Ausf As and Alkett taking up production of the StuG III Ausf B.

The monthly production figures for the Ausf A are given in table 1.

Alkett was at the time one of the seven companies involved in the production of the Panzer III with the Ausf G having gone into production at their factory in April 1940. To satisfy this supplementary order Alkett took 20 Pz III Ausf G (6/ZW) from the production line turning them into assault guns. They thus retained many features of the Pz III, including the escape hatches on either hull side. However, the running gear was still formatted for the narrow 360mm-wide track as used on the Daimler-Benz-produced Ausf A and was allocated a Fahrgestall Nummer in the 90401–90500 range. According to Walter Speilberger:

'The Ausf A designation was correctly applied because these converted Panzerkampfwagen chassis still possessed the 10-speed Maybach SRG 32 8 1 45 drive train.'

Sturmgeschütz III Ausf B

Built	Jun 1940–May 1941
No built	320
Fahrgestall Nummer	90101–90420
	90501–90550 (supplementary order for 50 Ausf B)
Manufacturer	Alkett
Chassis employed	6/ZW (Pz IIIG)
Weight	20.2 tons
Engine	Maybach HL120 TRM

The delay in instigating production of the Ausf B over and above the problems experienced at Daimler-Benz can be seen by the fact that 250 of this variant had been ordered as far back as February 1939, to follow on immediately after the completion of the contract with Daimler-Benz for the Ausf A, with Alkett as the designated manufacturer. According to the same memorandum of 13 October 1939 that led to the production of the first series of the StuG by Daimler-Benz, the second and third series, which were to be designated the Ausf B, were to begin in April 1940 with 250 to be built. At the time the memorandum was issued it was assumed that this second series would also be built by Daimler-Benz, but it had become apparent in the early months of 1940 that the firm was so swamped with the production of panzers, half-tracks and continuing repair work on damaged machines from the Polish Campaign that manufacture of the StuG had to be switched. It was transferred in its entirety to the company of Altmärkische Kettenwerk GmbH, at Berlin-Tegel, better known simply as Alkett. This company thus became the prime manufacturer of the assault gun until the end of the war, only being joined by a second company, Muhlenberg und Industrie AG (MIAG), when output of the type was ramped up to mass production with the Ausf G in February 1943. Alkett was thus the sole source of production of the 75mm

TABLE 1: Production of the Ausf A by Daimler-Benz

Date	Intended production	Accepted by Waffenamt	Produced by Daimler-Benz
Dec 1939	1	0	0
Jan 1940	1	1	1
Feb 1940	6	3	3
Mar 1940	10	6	6
Apr 1940	10	10	10
May 1940	10	10	10

TABLE 2: Production of the Ausf B by Alkett

Date	Intended production	Accepted by Waffenamt	Produced by Alkett	Comments
1940				
Jun	8	12	12	Start Ausf B Series 2
Jul	22	12	22	
Aug	32	10	20	Due to priority orders
Sep	36	29	29	
Oct	30	35	35	
Nov	36	35	35	
Dec	34	21	29	
1941				
Jan	36	44	36	
Feb	34	30	30	End of prod of Ausf B

L/24-armed StuG III until it was taken out of production in March 1942.

The first Sturmgeschütz Ausf B left the Alkett production line in June 1940 with construction of this mark lasting through to March 1941. The monthly production total of the Ausf B is detailed in table 2.

■ A new shock absorber with a metal sleeve replaced the bellows type of the Ausf A. This was retained on Alkett-manufactured StuGs through to the end of the conflict.
■ Introduction of a new drive sprocket with six spokes. This obtained on all Alkett-built StuG IIIs through to the Ausf G until replaced in March 1944.
■ A new track tensioner introduced with a non-overhanging spindle for protection.
■ A 40cm-wide track comprising of two grooves and a double-sided bar that would enable snow chevrons or cleats to be fitted in winter.

Sturmgeschütz Ausf C and D

Built	May and Sep 1940
No built	50 (Ausf C) and 150 (Ausf D)
Fahrgestall Nummer	90551–90600 (Ausf C) 90551–90750 (Ausf D)
Manufacturer	Alkett
Chassis employed	(Ausf C and D) 7/ZW Panzer III Ausf H
Weight	20.2 tons
Engine	Maybach HL120 TRM

The reason both of these marks are covered together is that there was little to tell them apart externally.

Combat experience had revealed the vulnerability of the direct vision port for the gunner's sight. This had proved to be a weak point in the frontal armour protection of the StuG III. The company of Krupp was issued with a contract to come up with a solution to providing the StuG with an alternative sighting system while eliminating the direct vision port. Their solution was to raise the sight by 80mm, such that it now projected through a new hatch in the roof of the vehicle which replaced the earlier two-part hatch. A section on the right side of this was cut out to allow the projection of the new gun sight above the hull roof. This periscope permitted 4 x magnification for the gunner and 10° of angle.

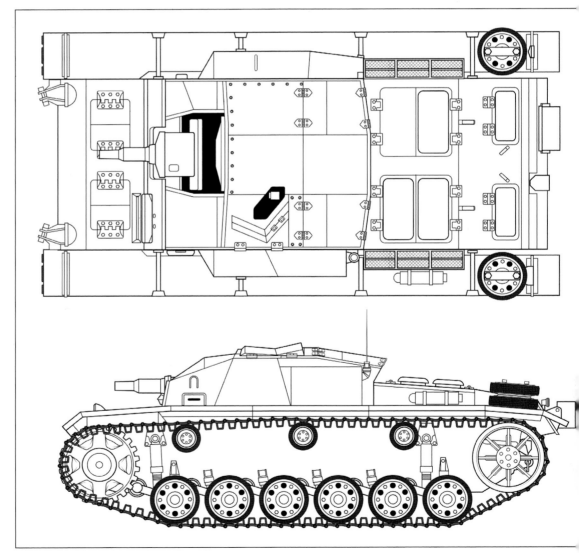

RIGHT StuG Ausf C.

(Mark Rolfe)

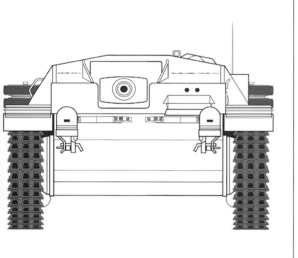

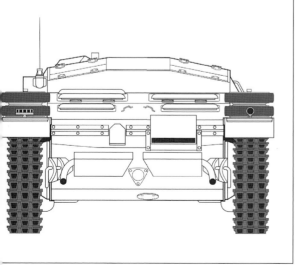

- Introduction of a new idler wheel with eight spokes. This obtained on all Alkett-built StuG IIIs through to the end of production in 1945.

- A new 40cm track link with two grooves and a double sidebar that permitted the fitting, when necessary, of snow cleats or a snow chevron. The open guide horn was retained.

- Introduced on the Ausf D was a wooden stowage rail that was mounted on three metal stilts and located on the left side of the StuG. This was to permit the single antenna mounted on the rear of the projecting radio compartment to be lowered when necessary.

- Subsequently this was also back-fitted on to all surviving earlier StuG marks.

- A number of Ausf Ds were 'tropicalised' for service in North Africa by the fitting of additional air filters outside the engine compartment. This was to reduce the high degree of wear and tear incurred by the inability of the normal filters to cope with the fine dust and subsequent reduction in efficiency of the engine. It was one of these Ausf Ds captured and evaluated by the British Army in the UK that forms the substance of Chapter 4 dealing with the short-barrelled StuGs.

- From the Ausf D onward all StuGs were outfitted with an MG34 to bolster the onboard crew armament of one MP38/40 SMG that was stowed on the rear wall of the fighting compartment.

Sturmgeschütz III Ausf E

Built	Oct 1941–Feb 1942
No built	272
Fahrgestall Nummer	90751–91036
Manufacturer	Alkett
Chassis employed	7/ZW Panzer III Ausf F
Weight	22 tons
Engine	Maybach HL120 TRM

The original order for the Ausf E was for 600 machines. However, this order was truncated at 272, with Alkett delivering the last StuG III with the 75mm L/24 weapon in February 1942. All machines built thereafter by Alkett, but still under the Ausf E contract, were finished with the longer-barrel 75mm StuK 40 L/43 main gun and re-designated the Ausf F. One Ausf E had been taken from the production line to be employed as a prototype for the trials of the L/43 gun as was another to trial the 105mm howitzer for the Sturmhaubitze prototype. This is addressed in more detail later in the text as is the use of 12 Ausf E chassis that were converted into Sturminfanteriegeschütz (SIG 33B).

■ The most important change in the Ausf E was the fitting of new and better radio equipment that at last allowed StuG battery and platoon commanders to

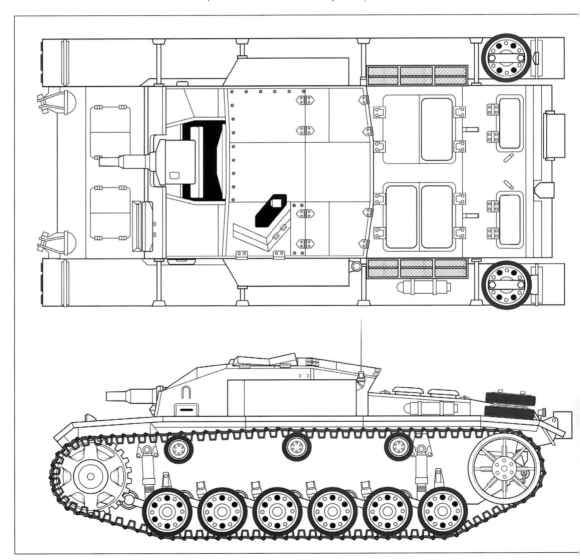

RIGHT StuG Ausf E.

(Mark Rolfe)

ABOVE StuG III Ausf E photographed at Jüterborg in 1941.

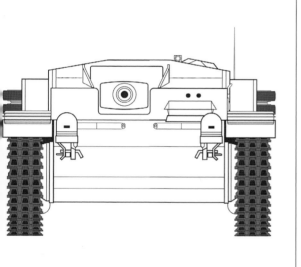

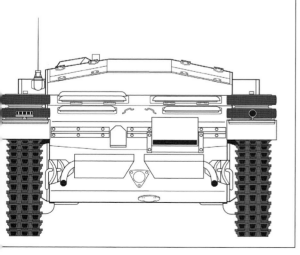

exercise control of their units from inside a StuG rather than employ the vulnerable light, one-ton command half-track – the Beobachtungskraftwagen 253 – which had been employed hitherto.

■ To that end, extra radio equipment was fitted into two larger, extended panniers located on either side of the StuG superstructure. A '10Wsh' 10W transmitter plus two UKW-Empf.h VHF receivers and a loudspeaker were added to a StuG that was intended to be employed as the platoon leader's command vehicle.

■ The Ausf E was equipped with two hinged radio antenna mounts on the left-hand and right-hand rear walls of their respective radio compartments. These folded down into two wooden stowage rails, each of which was mounted on three pairs of metal stilts. The middle pair of these rested on the penultimate screws of the air intake mesh.

■ An Army communication issued in December 1941 sanctioned the fitting of a welded retention bar across the front plate of the StuG behind which spare track links could be placed. This was ordered to be retrofitted on to all surviving earlier StuGs.

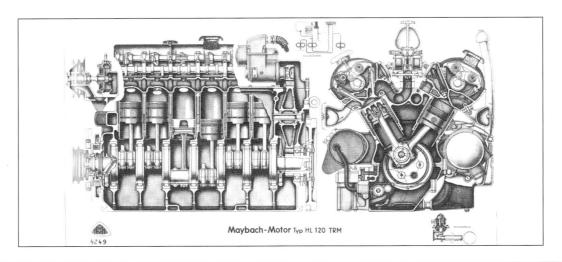

Maybach-Motor Typ HL 120 TRM

150MM STURMINFANTERIEGESCHÜTZ 33

The mounting of a sIG 33 150mm heavy howitzer support gun on a Panzer III chassis was a recommendation that flowed directly from the inadequate carriage of that weapon, firstly on a Panzer I then on a Panzer II chassis. The gun, which was an infantry support weapon, although heavy, was deemed to be most effective, but its limited range (its maximum being just 4.7km and being primarily horse drawn) precluded it from being able to support rapidly moving infantry assaults. The answer was to provide the gun with mobility. The mounting of 38 of these weapons on the Panzer I chassis permitted six sIG-Kompanien to be established and these were employed in the French Campaign and were effective in use, but the machine was hamstrung by the fact that it was much overloaded. Nonetheless, a number were still in service in 1943.

The second attempt to produce a self-propelled gun with the sIG 33 saw the employment of a Panzer II chassis, but unlike its predecessor wherein the gun had been mounted on top of the tank hull, on the new design the weapon was mounted within the hull albeit with major modifications to accommodate the gun's width as it was greater than that of the standard Panzer II. The design and construction by Alkett saw the hull of the Panzer II widened and lengthened. On this occasion just 12 test machines were built. Sent to North Africa in early 1942 they were not a success, with the chassis proving to be overloaded by the gun. Although aspects of the vehicle had proved to be useful in combat, a report sent back to Germany concluded that 'for any further production, it is considered necessary that the Panzer III chassis be selected'.

This is indeed what had happened even

ABOVE The first attempt to build a heavy infantry support gun on a tank chassis led to Alkett converting 38 Panzer IBs in February 1940. The body of the panzer was modified to carry the hefty 150mm sIG 33 L/11 infantry howitzer. This was protected by a three-sided box-shaped gun shield that was open at the top and rear. It was ready in time for service in the French Campaign, and it served in Russia with the very last example being lost in 1943. The chassis of the Panzer I was too weak to properly support such a weapon.

Totals of the short-barrelled Sturmgeschütz III produced between Jan 1940 and Feb 1942			
Date	Daimler-Benz	Alkett	
1940	30	182	These numbers correspond to the production of the Ausf A, B, C, D and E.
1941		532	
1942		90	
	30	804	

In many cases the number produced on a monthly basis either exceeded or did not meet the scheduled target goals. As an example of the former, in October 1941 the production goal was for 50 StuG III E to be produced whereas 71 were actually accepted by the Waffenamt. An example of the latter can be seen in the case of 32 Ausf Bs being the target for production in August 1940, with just 10 actually being built.

Manufacture of the StuG III armed with the 75mm L/24 ended in February 1942 with a total of 834 having been produced since January 1940.

before this report was received in Germany and had arisen in the course of a Führerkonferenz in September. From this Albert Speer, the Reich Armaments Minister, had noted down the main points concerning his conversation with Hitler who had observed that there was a need for 'a heavy gun mounted in a very heavily armoured vehicle firing mine-type ammunition capable of destroying houses with a few rounds' and that 'everything possible be done to ensure that 12, a minimum of 6 were produced within 14 days'. Alkett was commissioned for the task and employed a dozen refurbished Panzer III hulls for the project. These machines had been returned from the Front in a badly damaged state and had been rebuilt by Alkett. As time was of the essence the design was quite simple but nonetheless effective for the role envisaged, which was that of close infantry support in the fighting within Stalingrad. In Waffenamt production files these 12 machines were described as a 'one-time trial series mounted on rebuilt chassis'.

A box-shaped, fully enclosed superstructure was created. This comprised 80mm frontal armour and 50mm on the sides within which the 150mm howitzer was mounted on top of the Panzer III hull. The new machine had a crew of 5 and carried 30 rounds of the 150mm ammunition. The nature of the design – that of a box – also permitted the fitting of an integral MG34 machine gun to the right of the main gun, something, of course, which was not possible on the standard StuG III. The combat

ABOVE A second, albeit unsuccessful, attempt to mount the same 150mm weapon on a lengthened Panzer II chassis was made in late 1941 with 12 being built before production ceased. They were used in North Africa. This in turn led to the third attempt to produce a self-propelled 150mm howitzer, but this time based on a Panzer III chassis. The gun was housed in an enclosed fighting compartment – as with the StuG III – with 24 being built between December 1941 and October 1942. It was referred to as a Sturmgeschütz.

weight of the machine was 21 tons. These were committed to combat with two Sturmgeschütz Abteilungen in the Stalingrad fighting and were lost there by the time Sixth Army surrendered in January 1943. A second batch of 12 was built employing new-build StuG chassis and committed to the fighting in southern Russia. The last of this second tranche was reported lost by the 23rd Panzer Division (the unit it was operating with) in October 1943. A captured surviving machine is on display at the Russian Tank Museum at Kubinka.

Chapter Three

Long-barrelled StuG III Ausf F–G (SdKfz 142/1)

A new and improved longer-barrelled 75mm L/43 and L/48 main gun was fitted to the Sturmgeschütz in 1942 so it could deal effectively with the new generation of Soviet tanks first encountered in Russia in 1941. The L/48 weapon equipped the assault gun through to war's end in 1945.

OPPOSITE **A long-barrelled StuG III rumbles through the city of Lappeenranta in south-east Finland on its way to the Front, July 1944.** *(SA-kuva – Finnish Armed Forces photograph)*

Work had begun on the design and development of a longer gun for the StuG III by the Krupp Company even before the outbreak of war. This had led to the creation of the 75mm L/41 weapon, which was accepted in July 1940 after testing. However, on 20 November 1941 the Führer cancelled the order, decreeing that the Sturmgeschütz required an even longer gun with increased muzzle velocity to enable it to deal with enemy vehicles encountered on the Eastern Front. The actual order for this new weapon was as follows.

The Führer has, due to thorough appreciation of the value of the Sturmgeschütz, ordered the following:

BELOW StuG Ausf F.
(Mark Rolfe)

■ The armour is to be strengthened on newly produced Sturmgeschütz without regard to the disadvantages of increased weight and the resulting loss of speed.

■ The Sturmgeschütz must receive a long-barrelled 75mm gun with a higher muzzle velocity. The advantage over new types of enemy tanks can only be regained in this way.

Whereas Krupp had developed the now cancelled 75mm L/41 gun, the contract to develop the 'long-barrelled 75mm gun' as demanded by the German leader was issued to the company of Rheinmetall-Borsig with the instruction to produce three experimental 75mm Kanone L/46 guns as soon as possible. Indeed, the Heereswaffenamt was to publish a document at the beginning of December, which anticipated production of the first 10

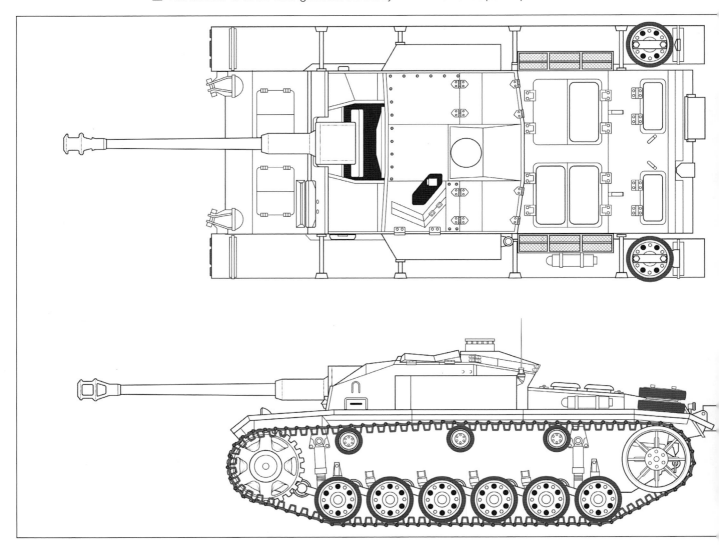

such weapons in February 1942. On 16 March 1942 it was ordered that the weapon be re-designated as the 75mm Sturmkanone (abbreviated to StuK) 40 L/43. The production life of this weapon was short – precluding the three experimental weapons produced in February 1942 – just 285 L/43 weapons were manufactured for equipping the assault gun before it was superseded by the 75mm L/48 main gun.

Following the decision to terminate production of the Ausf E after 234 examples of the 600 on order, the remainder were contracted to be equipped with the 75mm L/43 and re-designated the Ausf F. This meant that the 280 75mm L/24 weapons that had been produced to fulfil the contract for the Ausf E were now redundant. Fertile minds found a use for them, however,

with 190 being used to create a new variant of the SdKfz 251 – the Army's standard 3-ton Schützenpanzerwagen (SPW) – as a fire-support vehicle with the designation 251/9. The remainder found their way to equipping a new variant of the eight-wheeled SdKfz 231, subsequently designated the SdKfz 233.

The very last of the short-barrelled StuGs left the Alkett production line in March 1942. The long-barrelled StuGs – be they carrying the L/43 (Ausf F) or the L/48 (Ausf F/8 and G) – were designated SdKfz 142/1.

Sturmgeschütz Ausf F L/43 main gun

Built	Mar–Sep 1942
No built	359/366 (this latter figure indicates total number produced with chassis diverted for other purposes)
Fahrgestall Nummer	91037–91400
Manufacturer	Alkett
Chassis employed	7/ZW Panzer III Ausf F
Weight	23.2 tons
Engine	Maybach HL120 TRM

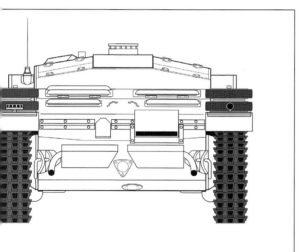

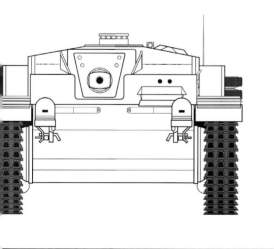

The new, longer-barrelled Sturmgeschütz that first left Alkett's production line in March 1942 was unchanged from the previous Ausf E, excepting those aspects required to facilitate the fitting and working of the new, longer gun.

BELOW A StuG III Ausf F in Russia, 1942. At the time of its introduction in the early summer of 1942, this variant of the StuG was the most powerfully armed German AFV in the East apart from the Panzer IV F2 mounting the same weapon. Note that it is using T-34 track links as added protection across the lower glacis.

The 75mm StuK40 L/43 gun was built between March and May 1942 with a total of 122 being produced in that time. It was the carriage of the L/43 weapon that identified the StuG III as an Ausf F.

Main features added to StuG III Ausf F over production run

■ The superstructure front on either side of the new gun mounting was changed with the opening for the armament being enlarged to ensure a traverse of 20º. This was realised by the reduction of the angle of the armour on either side of the mantlet opening.

■ The most noticeable visual change apart from the new main gun was the fitting of a more effective fan for the rapid evacuation of the fumes from the main gun after it had been fired. This was moved from the wall at the rear of the fighting compartment to directly above the breech of the main gun and was mounted on a small raised platform. This feature was to be found on all F and F/8 models of the StuG.

■ New ammunition bins added for the longer shells.

■ Weight of the new Ausf F increased to 23.2 tons.

■ The Nebelkerzenabwurfvorrichtung – the smoke candle launcher located on the right-hand rear of the StuG, and which had been a feature of all marks of the vehicle since the Ausf A – was deleted.

■ As from June 1942, and at Hitler's behest, the frontal armour of the StuG Ausf F was

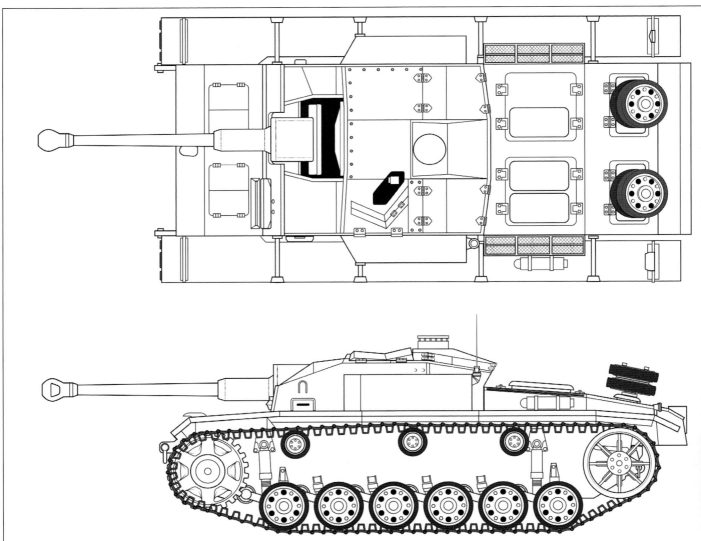

raised from 50mm to 80mm. First fitted on the last 11 StuGs produced in June 1942, this saw a slab of 30mm armour welded to the upper and lower nose plates of the hull and the forward 50mm base plate.

■ From August 1942 the angle of the amour on either side of the mantlet housing was increased so that there was now an unbroken transition from the top of the front plate to the forward edge of the superstructure roof. Clearly this had been seen as necessary, as StuG crews using the earlier production Ausf Fs had found the reduction of the armour had created a shot and had of their accord resorted to a field expedient of employing concrete to do the same.

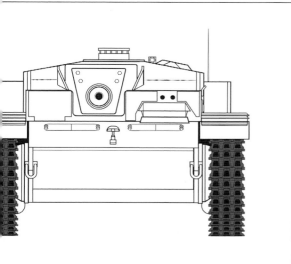

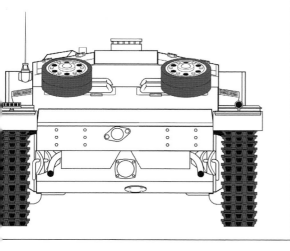

■ The two armoured cowled headlights on the front of the hull were replaced by a single Notek light mounted at its centre.

Sturmgeschütz Ausf F/8, L/48 main gun

It is clear that the 75mm StuK40 L/43 was only ever seen as an interim weapon, with the L/48 weapon being regarded as the definitive long-barrelled gun intended for the StuG III. The first model to mount this new weapon was an Ausf F, re-designated the F/8, as it was built from the outset with this new gun. The first F/8 model left Alkett's production line in September 1942 and continued to be manufactured through to December of that year when it was replaced by the much modified StuG Ausf G. Design and manufacture of the new weapon (coverage of which is included in Chapter 5 Anatomy) had been undertaken by Rheinmetall-Borsig with the first 78 of the L/48 gun being produced in June 1942 with a further 88 being manufactured in September.

Built	Sep–Dec 1942
No built	250
Fahrgestall Nummer	91401–91650
Manufacturer	Alkett
Chassis employed	8/ZW Ausf J (see below)
Weight	23.2 tons
Engine	Maybach HL120 TRM

Main features added to StuG III Ausf F/8 over production run

■ Delays in the supply of the 8/ZW-derived hulls perforce led Alkett to employ hulls intended for the PzKpfw III Ausf L and M manufactured by them and instead use them to manufacture the StuG III Ausf F/8. In consequence, it was decided that Alkett would cease production of the PzKpfw III in September 1942. Thereafter all ZW hulls were to be employed solely for the expanded production of the StuG III Ausf G that began in December 1942.

■ A distinctive feature that permitted easy identification of the F/8 was that the two front towing points were created by extending the hull sidewalls beyond the front plate and holes were drilled in them on either side.

- ■ Rear hull armour thickness increased to 50mm.
- ■ As a consequence of delays in the delivery of the 'acorn' shape muzzle brake, a number of the last of the Ausf F off the production line and the first few (number imprecise) of the new Ausf F/8 were fitted with the same round ball-shaped muzzle brake as found on the PzKpfw IVF2. Once these delivery problems were overcome all F/8s and all 75mm-armed StuGs built thereafter through to the war's end employed the acorn-shaped muzzle brake.
- ■ As of October 1942, welding of the additional 30mm armour to the front of the StuG was superseded by the same thickness of armour plates being attached to their respective positions on the front of the hull by having holes drilled into them and then being attached by heavy bolts.
- ■ A machine-gun shield was trialled with a number of StuG F/8s. They were placed in front of the loader's station and had to be raised to provide a degree of cover. The loader placed the MG34 that was carried within the hull inside the space on the shield in order to fire. This was not deemed to be the best solution to close-in defence as the loader had to expose the upper part of his body to fire the weapon. Nonetheless, this became a standard fitting on all StuG Gs

from December 1942 and was back-fitted on to all surviving F/8s in early 1943.

- ■ The pivoting radio mounts were replaced on the F/8 with fixed mounts, these being mounted in the same position as previously.
- ■ A protective mesh cage was fitted over the gunner's sight on the roof of the StuG.
- ■ On the rear engine deck the larger openings were now protected by armoured cowlings.

Total number of all Sturmgeschütz III Ausf A through F/8 produced between January 1940 and December 1942 amounted to 1,536 vehicles. All were manufactured by Alkett except for the first 30 Ausf As built by Daimler-Benz. The numbers in brackets refer to the acceptances by the Heereswaffenamt from the Alkett factory. It was not always the case during StuG production from 1940 to 1945 that the number produced equated to the number received.

MASS PRODUCTION
Sturmgeschütz III Ausf G

Built	Dec 1942–Apr 1945
No built	8,416
Fahrgestall Nummer	Alkett – 91651–94250 and 105001–108920
	MIAG – 95001–97586
Manufacturer(s)	Alkett, MIAG
Chassis employed	StuG III
Weight	24 tons
Engine	Maybach HL120 TRM

As part of the general expansion of Germany's war industries in 1942, a major increase in the production of the Sturmgeschütz III had been planned with the introduction of a new mark. This major redesign of the machine encompassed many of the comments and insights provided by the frontline users – StuG crews being encouraged, as were panzer crews, to pass on observations and ideas that could improve the vehicle – allied to changes to the design to facilitate the easier production of much larger numbers of the vehicle. This is addressed in detail in Chapters 4 and 5 Anatomy of the StuG III.

Date 1942	Number produced	Built by	General remarks
Mar	3 (3)	Alkett	Start of Ausf F
Apr	36 (36)	Alkett	Conversion to the 75mm L/43
May	79 (79)	Alkett	
Jun	70 (70)	Alkett	Start of equipping the Ausf F with the 75mm L/48 gun and extra 30mm armour plate to become the F/8
Jul	60 (60)	Alkett	
Aug	80 (80)	Alkett	
Sep	70 (70)	Alkett	Actual start of F/8 production
Oct	84 (84)	Alkett	
Nov	100 (100)	Alkett	
Dec	120 (120)	Alkett	Switch over to Ausf G
1942 total	**702 (702)**	**Alkett**	

The Sturmgeschütz III Ausf G entered production in December 1942. It was to remain so substantially unchanged through to April 1945 when all production of the type ceased. With the introduction of this new Ausführung, output of the StuG III increased substantially at Alkett with the company delivering 130 of the new mark in January 1943 alone. By October 1943, 255 (other sources quote 270) StuGs left its production lines. However, the high point in this company's output was achieved in January 1945 when 320 assault guns left the production lines. This planned expansion in the output of the StuG III also embraced the company of Mühlenbau und Industrie AG (hereafter MIAG) of Braunschweig, which was drafted in as a second source of production. MIAG had been producing the Panzerkampfwagen III since October 1941 and continued building this medium panzer until told to switch production to the StuG III towards the end of 1942. MIAG produced its first Ausf G in February 1943. In January 1944 it manufactured 150 StuGs, this number representing the largest total produced by the company in any one month through to April 1945.

By the war's end Alkett had produced 5,773 and MIAG 2,643 StuGs respectively of the Ausf G model, with 8,416 of these having been accepted by the Waffenamt.

ABOVE A line-up of very early StuG Ausf Gs destined for service with StuGAbt 226. The primary identification feature of the very earliest examples of this new assault gun variant was the sharply angled side-plate of the new fighting compartment. This was wider than on all previous StuG variants.

Alkett: The first 200 of the Ausf Gs built by this company employed the 200 surplus F/8 hulls left over from the production of that model, which had ceased in December. This posed no problem as the hulls were identical.

MIAG: In the course of manufacturing StuG IIIs during 1943, this company derived its hulls from a number of sources:

1) StuGs produced by MIAG that employed the hulls of the discontinued PzKpfw III Ausf N that they had manufactured (the last PzKpfw III Ausf N was produced by MIAG in August 1943).
2) StuGs produced by MIAG that employed the hulls of the PzKpfw III Ausf M that they were manufacturing until the type was discontinued (the last PzKpfw III Ausf M was produced by MIAG in February 1943).

Both 1) and 2) totalled 98 tank hulls, which were used to build StuG III Ausf Gs between April and November 1943.

3) StuGs built on the discontinued PzKpfw III Ausf M built by Maschinenfabrik Augsberg-Nürnberg AG (hereafter MAN) were delivered to MIAG in running condition. These arrived at the MIAG works with 30mm secondary hull armour already welded on and the deep wading muffler carried on the upper rear hull.

4) StuGs constructed on the purpose-built 9/10 ZW chassis by MIAG for the StuG III Ausf G.

Main features added to Ausf G over production run

■ From April 1943, assault guns delivered by Alkett had 80mm armour. This featured on all StuGs delivered by MIAG from July 1943 employing the purpose-built StuG chassis.

■ Those StuGs manufactured by MIAG that employed chassis constructed upon the now discontinued PzKpfw III required the extra frontal armour of 30mm (raising it to 80mm) to still be bolted on to the hulls as had been the case with the StuG F/8. For example, May/June 1943 saw 57 PzKpfw IIIs finished in this manner.

■ First series of Ausf G built by Alkett had a bend in the track guard to accommodate the new larger and longer superstructure.

■ Two three-barrelled launchers for smoke grenades were fitted on both Alkett and MIAG StuGs for just three months between February and May 1943 before they were discontinued (as was the case with the new Panther D).

■ MIAG workers fitted the new cupola on the

BELOW StuG Ausf G.
(Mark Rolfe)

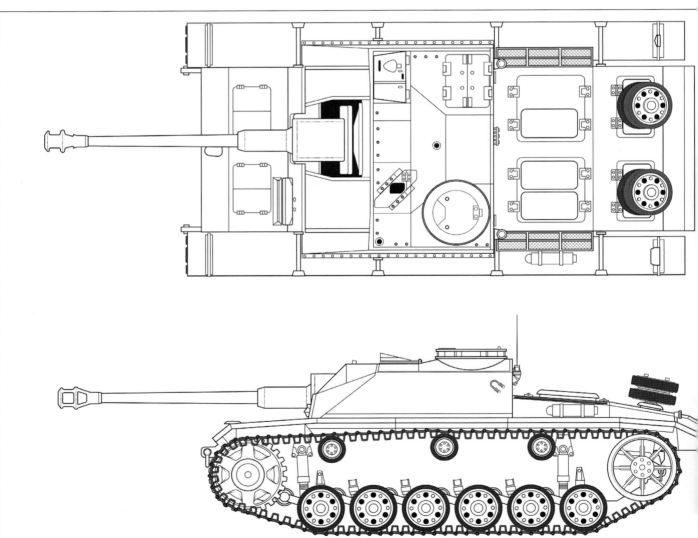

StuG superstructure incorrectly. The rear of the cupola was placed facing forward.

■ From April 1943 all StuG III Ausf Gs were to be fitted with mountings along the side of the hull to permit 5mm sheets of steel to be hung, intended to defeat Soviet anti-tank rifle shells. In many cases, however, delays resulted in the skirts being fitted after new-build vehicles had reached the Front. Surviving Ausf F and F/8 StuGs were also fitted with these skirts (*Schürzen*).

■ In July 1944 the attachment of the skirts was changed with the *Schürzen* now being hung from triangular attachment points on angled profile railing.

■ *Zimmerit* (see box-out text) was added by Alkett from November 1943 and MIAG from December 1943. The former employed a waffle pattern (this can be seen on the Finnish StuG Ausf G in Chapter 6 StuG III walk-around) and the latter, a mesh-type pattern.

■ Both companies fitted railings around the engine deck at different times to enable crew to store various items. Alkett began to do so in November 1943 and MIAG in May 1944.

■ A Notek blackout light was mounted on the centre of the upper bow plate. This continued to be fitted in this position up to July 1944.

■ Two types of new armoured circular ventilator covers were fitted: from December 1942 through to February 1943 an armoured cover was located between the commander's cupola and the loader's hatch; from the end of February 1943 until the end of the war this cover was relocated to the centre of the rear vertical superstructure plate.

■ From December 1942 Alkett added a bracket to carry spare track links across the rear vertical superstructure plate. MIAG did so from the start of its production of the Ausf G in February 1943. This was a standard fitting on the Ausf G through to war's end.

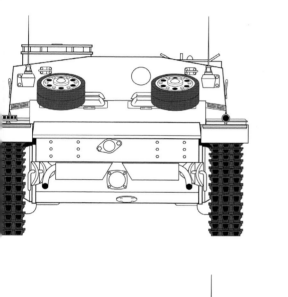

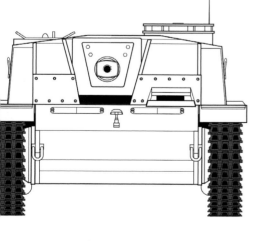

■ In the light of the scarcity of rubber, return rollers with rubber tyres were replaced by Alkett from December 1943 with a steel six-ribbed roller with holes between each. Replaced in January by a new roller with no ribs and six equidistantly placed drain holes. MIAG introduced an all-steel, six-spoked roller in December 1943, which remained in production to the end of the war. However, it was ordered that outstanding stocks of rubber-tyred return rollers continue to be fitted until supplies were exhausted. This accounts for new production StuG IIIs still employing such return rollers through to 1944.

■ Radio antenna fitted in rigid mounts on the left and right of the rear bulkhead of the fighting compartment.

■ Machine-gun shield replaced as from July 1944 by a Rundumfeuer – an externally mounted MG34 located in front of the loader's hatch and fired from within the hull. This was to provide 360° protection. However, this did not become a regular feature on either Alkett or MIAG StuG IIIs

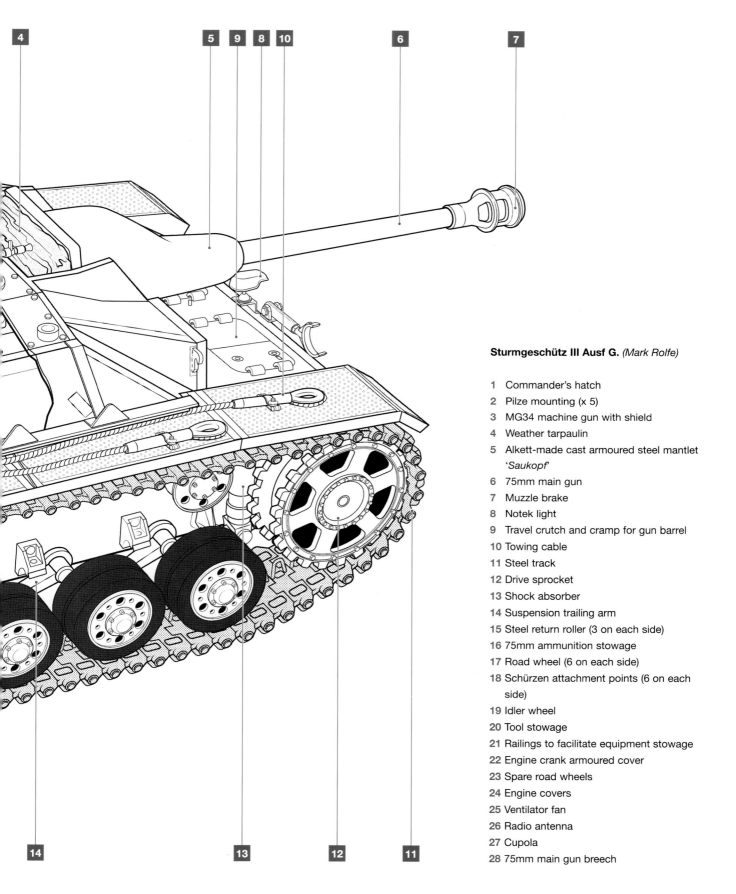

Sturmgeschütz III Ausf G. *(Mark Rolfe)*

1 Commander's hatch
2 Pilze mounting (x 5)
3 MG34 machine gun with shield
4 Weather tarpaulin
5 Alkett-made cast armoured steel mantlet *'Saukopf'*
6 75mm main gun
7 Muzzle brake
8 Notek light
9 Travel crutch and cramp for gun barrel
10 Towing cable
11 Steel track
12 Drive sprocket
13 Shock absorber
14 Suspension trailing arm
15 Steel return roller (3 on each side)
16 75mm ammunition stowage
17 Road wheel (6 on each side)
18 Schürzen attachment points (6 on each side)
19 Idler wheel
20 Tool stowage
21 Railings to facilitate equipment stowage
22 Engine crank armoured cover
23 Spare road wheels
24 Engine covers
25 Ventilator fan
26 Radio antenna
27 Cupola
28 75mm main gun breech

until October 1944. Even then, many StuGs were seen equipped with the fitting and its angled shield, but without the machine gun.

■ From December 1943 Alkett replaced the box-type mantlet of the StuG Ausf G with a new cast armour steel mantlet made in the shape of a *Saukopf* (or pig's head). MIAG retained the original box-type mantlet, fitting it to the end of the conflict.

■ Provision for a second MG34 was included in a coaxial mount from MIAG in May 1944 and Alkett in their cast mantlet from June 1944 to the end of the war. Once again provision for carriage of the same was made but not all were fitted.

■ It was intended to fit a Nahverteidigungswaffe – a close-in defence weapon – on the roof of the fighting compartment, but as this was not always available for fitting, the roof opening was sealed over with a cover, either from the inside or the outside. From September/October 1944 the opening was permanently sealed by a cover on the roof of the StuG, apart from on those very few machines that were fitted with the device.

■ From December 1943 a tarpaulin was fitted

between the mantlet and the front of the fighting compartment to provide protection from inclement weather.

■ The requirement as set out in Army Technical Order Number 422 of 1 July 1944 was that 'Pilze' mounts be affixed by welding to the roof of the fighting compartment. Whereas some machines were given three of these mounts, in October 1944 it was ordered that the StuG would receive five – one to be welded to each corner of the fighting compartment roof and the fifth to be placed in its middle. This was to enable a 2-ton jib crane to be erected if necessary.

■ In June 1944 a travel crutch and clamp was provided to accommodate the gun barrel by MIAG. Alkett followed suit in July. This was mounted in the centre of the upper bow plate in the position formerly occupied by the Notek light. The position of the Notek light was shifted to the right of the travel crutch.

■ From December 1944 a track pin deflector was welded to the hull side of all new-build StuGs inside the idler wheel to prevent track pins from shearing off when in contact with

RIGHT The crutch and clamp to accommodate the gun barrel during transit was one of several design additions made to the Ausf G, initially by MIAG and followed in July 1944 by Alkett. This Ausf G was captured by American troops in the Ardennes in the winter offensive of 1944.

the hull armour. This modification was to be back-fitted on to all older serving assault guns.

■ In August 1944 a new final drive was fitted on to StuGs leaving the production lines. The growth in the weight of the assault gun – it had become increasingly nose-heavy as more frontal armour had been added, in addition to the extra weight of the longer gun – had led to increasing stress being placed on to the machine's final drives, which had originally been designed for the lighter Panzer III. As with the Panther, the problematic final drive led to a lot of breakdowns of StuGs, many of which could not be recovered and had perforce to be abandoned.

■ Although not a factory modification, an increasingly seen alteration on StuG IIIs serving on the Eastern Front – particularly the Ausf Gs – was the addition of concrete by crews in the field to bolster protection of the armour on the front of the superstructure.

■ The official view was that this added no real protection to the StuG, but nonetheless it was seen having been added to the end of the war.

Alkett was bombed for the first time in November 1943. This impacted on production of the StuG III such that in December just 24 vehicles were produced. The factory was bombed again in January 1944. MIAG was the recipient of more raids with these occurring in February, March, April, August, October and November 1944. The impact of these raids are reflected in the output figures.

ABOVE MIAG became only the second manufacturer of the Sturmgeschütz when it began production in February 1942 of the Ausf G. This example produced by them was built with the later, more extreme angled side-plate, and is being delivered already fitted with the framework to mount the *Schürzen* armoured side-skirts.

Sturmgeschütz Ausf G production, Jan 1943–Apr 1945						
Month	Alkett			MIAG		
	1943	1944	1945	1943	1944	1945
Jan	130	102	320	0	125	71
Feb	130	59	152	10	137	37
Mar	147	144	220	50	120	15
Apr	128	194	48	100	100	
May	140	255		120	80	
Jun	155	200		120	145	
Jul	161	236		120	135	
Aug	171	232		120	80	
Sep	205	265		140	100	
Oct	257	253		138	72	
Nov	98	251		130	110	
Dec	121	361		120	91	
Total StuG III Ausf G production – 7,721						

Sturmhaubitze III Ausf G SdKfz 142/2

Built	Oct 1942–Feb 1945
No built	1,299
Fahrgestall Nummer	92151–108920
Manufacturer	Alkett
Chassis employed	StuG III
Weight	24 tons
Engine	Maybach HL120 TRM

In consequence of the need to field more machines with guns big enough to defeat the Soviet T-34 and tanks of the KV series first encountered in Russia in the summer of 1941, the reality was that the introduction of the StuG III Ausf F and F/8 in 1942, and the Ausf G in 1943, saw these variants of the StuG increasingly employed as tank destroyers. Being cheaper to manufacture than conventional tanks and their relative ease of production when compared to them, it is unsurprising that they came to be seen as a means of bolstering, in the short term, the total numbers of AFVs employed by the Army and the burgeoning Waffen SS. Indeed, this was both essential and inevitable given the very small number of panzers that were serviceable on the Eastern Front at the beginning of 1943.

However, this was not appreciated by any means by the infantry for whom, as we have seen, the StuG was designed to aid. The diversion of this machine to tank-killing duties and also service with panzer divisions and the Waffen SS had seen the number of assault guns made available to aid the infantry decline substantially. It was thus recognised that something had to be done to once again provide the infantry with its own tracked artillery support weapon. To that end

RIGHT Entering production with Alkett in the spring of 1943 was the Sturmhaubitze – a StuG III Ausf G mounting a 105mm howitzer. They mainly served in mixed formations with the standard, 75mm-equipped StuG IIIs.

discussion had been ongoing about developing new assault artillery, and indeed this had been mooted in a report on tank and other weapons production as early as 2 December 1941 when it was recognised that: '. . . a howitzer mounted in a vehicle, as similar in construction to the Sturmgeschütz as possible, was deemed necessary for the effective engagement of soft targets, including those behind cover'.

The same report identified that a Sturmgeschütz III would be equipped with an 105mm L/28 leichte Feldhaubitze (LH) to fulfil this need. Apart from the mounting of this new weapon and the internal changes to accommodate the different ammunition it used, the new assault howitzer would be externally identical to the standard StuG III Ausf G.

A prototype Sturmhaubitze on an Ausf E chassis was constructed in October 1941 with 12 Versuchserie (trials series) to follow, produced by Alkett (who would subsequently become the sole manufacturer of this machine), completing 5 in December 1941, 5 in January 1942 and 2 in February 1942. A slippage in the production schedule was due to the late deliveries of the modified 105mm howitzers resulting in the prototype emerging only in March 1942. This was based on an Ausf F chassis. Although figures vary it is thought that a further 17 Versuchserie were constructed by Alkett before they began series production in March 1943. These 17 trials machines were built employing StuG III Ausf B to E chassis that had been returned to Alkett from the Front for refurbishment between October and December 1941, and May and June 1942.

It was not until October 1941 that Albert Speer, Reich Armaments Minister, was able to present an example of a trial Sturmhaubitze for the Führer's inspection. The German leader expressed his satisfaction with the design some days later in a conference on 13 October wherein he stated that he thought this 'was an ideal solution'. He demanded that provision be made in the production schedule of the StuG at Alkett for the manufacture of 12 of these machines per month. In that same month, the 3rd Batterie of Sturmgeschütz-Abteilung 185 operating with Army Group North had received 9 of the 17 trials Sturmhaubitze for combat assessment. First seeing combat on 22 November 1942, all had

been lost in the very intensive fighting by the year's end. Notwithstanding their total loss, the Sturmhaubitze had been well received by the artillery.

In the meantime, it was decided to employ new-build Ausf G chassis for the Sturmhaubitze with production beginning properly in March 1943 (more technical details are addressed in Chapters 4 and 5, Anatomy of the StuG III) following the initial issue of a contract for 200. Although 20 were planned for in March only 10 were actually manufactured, with 34 in April rising to 45 in May. Production was irregular throughout the remainder of 1943 due to delivery problems with Rheinmetal-Borsig who built the howitzers. Nonetheless, the original contract was fulfilled by the end of the year. Production continued with the very last Sturmhaubitze leaving Alkett's factory in April 1945, with some 1,299 being built.

Monthly production figures for the Sturmhaubitze 142				
Month	1942	1943	1944	1945
Jan		3	26	71
Feb		0	54	24
Mar		10	56	49
Apr		34	58	48
May		45	46	
Jun		30	100	
Jul		25	92	
Aug		5	110	
Sept		10	119	
Oct	9	11	100	
Nov		4	102	
Dec		30	40	
Total production of Sturmhaubitze 142 = 1,311 units				

Main features added to Sturmhaubitze 142 over production run

- New, cast *Saukopf* mantlet introduced on all Alkett-built assault howitzers as from October 1943.
- Aperture in cast mantlet for fitting an MG34 from June 1943. However, the decision to delete the mantlet on the 105mm howitzer as from September 1944 saw Alkett discontinue with the co-axial machine gun and thus the aperture in the *Saukopfblende*.

Chapter Four

Anatomy of the StuG III Ausf A–E

The anatomy description of the StuG III in this chapter owes much to an evaluation report produced by the British School of Tank Technology on an Ausf D captured in North Africa in 1943. This was one of a small number of assault guns modified for employment in that theatre of war.

OPPOSITE **The crew of a StuG III Ausf C pauses in the Russian countryside during the opening days of Operation 'Barbarossa', July 1941.** (*Bundesarchiv*)

Over the course of its production life, which lasted from January 1940 through to March 1945, the various models of the StuG were built in a number of series employing differing chassis of the ZW/Panzer III upon which it was based and that were in production at the time. The details of these are listed in the table below. Although Daimler-Benz was responsible for the production of the Ausf A, the second small batch of the Ausf A and all short-barrelled models thereafter were built by the firm of Alkett. The MIAG Company (Mühlenbau und Industrie AG) only began manufacturing the StuG III with the Ausf G, the first 10 of which they built in February 1943. The long-barrelled StuGs beginning with the F model are addressed in a separate section later in this chapter.

Ausführung designation	Series No/ ZW No	Panzer III Ausf designation
Ausf A		PzKpfw III Ausf F 2nd product batch
	1/ZW	PzKpfw III Ausf F
Ausf B	2/ZW	PzKpfw III Ausf H
Ausf C	3a/ZW	PzKpfw III Ausf F
Ausf D	3b/ZW	PzKpfw III Ausf H
Ausf E	4/ZW	PzKpfw III Ausf H

■ In all cases, although the bases of the StuG chassis were derived from that of a model of a Panzer III, they were modified to suit the design of the StuG excepting those occasions when PzKpfw III chassis were employed or modified/converted. When this is the case this will be pointed out.

Much of the more detailed aspects of the description of the interior of the Sturmgeschütz III that follow is derived from a British Army report on a captured Sturmgeschütz III Ausf D, Fahrgestall Nummer 90 683 of Sonderverband 288 (Special Operations Unit 288), captured in North Africa. This formation was raised in Potsdam and was prepared specifically for service in Africa. Organised as a Panzerjäger (tank destroyer company) it also included a platoon of Sturmgeschütz Ausf Ds. The formation arrived in Libya as an Army unit and was later renamed Panzer-Grenadier Regiment Afrika.

This captured StuG was shipped back to England where it was extensively examined by an evaluation team at the School of Tank Technology. The document produced in consequence was dated October 1943. This StuG was one of 150 Ausf Ds built by Alkett between May and September 1941. Of interest is the short history of the vehicle posted in the report. It states that the:

'. . . very first journey entered into the log book of the new vehicle was made on 20 August 1941 from Zinna – in the Berlin area. . . . It then left Germany for Greece (Koropi) between 16 September and 13 October 1941. From Greece it travelled to Fusaro, where it remained until having completed a total mileage of 682 (1,099km). After this, journeys were not regularly entered up. Between March and May 1942 the unit moved to the Middle East. By 28 June 1942 approximately 1,400 miles had been completed. At 1,050 miles the engine was changed. A pencilled note in the maintenance record book states that 56 rounds were fired on 27 May 1942 at Bir Hacheim and 62 rounds on 31 May 1942 and 118 rounds on 11 June 1942 at Acroma.'

General dimensions of the StuG Ausf D

Length: 18ft 0in
Width: 9ft 8in
Height: 6ft 4in

OPPOSITE Sturmgeschütz III Ausf D, Fahrgestall Nummer 90 683, was captured in North Africa and evaluated in England at the School of Tank Technology. It was one of three sent to the theatre as part of Sonderverband 288 (Special Operations Unit 288). Missing are the four additional air filters added to the StuG before it was despatched to the North African theatre. The additional empty brackets fitted to carry them can be seen above the third return roller. The rack extending across the rear of the hull was to carry water and petrol jerricans. On the right and below the rack can be seen the armoured smoke candle holder.

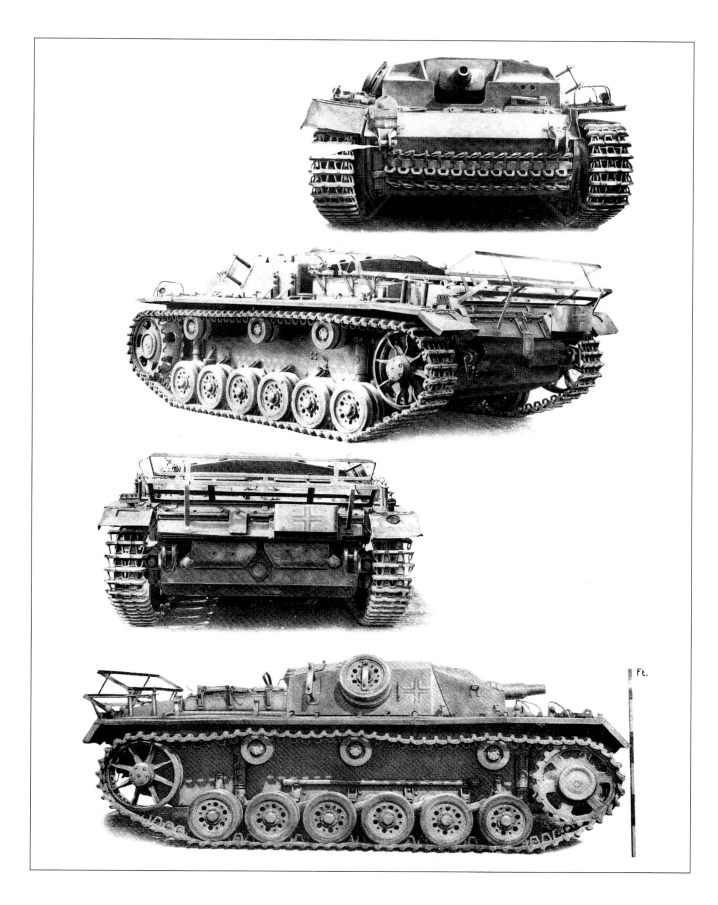

Ft.

Hull exterior – StuG Ausf D

The main lower hull of the StuG III Ausf D is a similar assembly to that used on the Panzer III, except that the tail plates are not the same thickness as the nose plates and are only 30mm thick.

The British report notes that no escape hatches were fitted in the hull sides, owing to the fact that the ZW hull employed on this model was a modified example based on that of the PzKpfw III Ausf H. Indeed, the only StuG IIIs fitted with escape hatches in the hull sides were on those chassis originally destined for the PzKpfw III, but diverted and completed as assault guns and this occurred rarely. The first occasion came about with StuGs of the second production batch built between June and September 1940, where the chassis of PzKpfw III Ausf F was mated to the superstructure of the StuG Ausf B. The escape hatches on the Panzer III hull were welded shut. The only other occasion when this occurred is covered in the second section on the StuG Ausf G when 57 Panzer III Ausf J to M were converted by MIAG into assault guns. But as with the Ausf As, the escape hatches were welded shut. Although the British evaluation team were aware that the StuG employed a PzKpfw III chassis, it seems they were not aware that it was modified for use on the assault gun, and that not all features of the PzKpfw III hull were carried over, such as the escape hatches.

The rear of the upper hull, while similar to that on the PzKpfw III, is sloped at a greater angle – that is, at 30° to the vertical.

The fighting compartment of the PzKpfw III was replaced by a squat non-rotating assembly that was bolted to the lower hull. The whole of the fighting compartment was detachable, which was necessary to allow remedial work to be done on the main armament. To facilitate this the turret roof was detachable, being held by countersunk screws to strips welded on the inside of the top of the turret walls.

Nine-millimetre plates sloping at an angle of 30° to the vertical 30mm turret sides are employed, apparently to increase the protection against hollow charge projectiles and to eliminate the possibility of damage to the top run of the track through high explosive (HE) strikes on the turret sides. On all models from the Ausf A through to the Ausf F/8 the rear superstructure armour was sloped backwards

The front cover plate of the gun recuperator mechanism appears to be a forging of 50mm minimum thickness, retained by four set screws screwed in from the rear.

Armour

The different thicknesses of the armour of the StuG III Ausf D is presented here together with the angles at which each respective plate of armour was fitted. Note that reference to the 'angle of plate' given is the angle between the plate surface and the vertical, which is equal to the 'angle of impact' for horizontal attack.

BELOW Armour plate thickness, profile and sectional view.

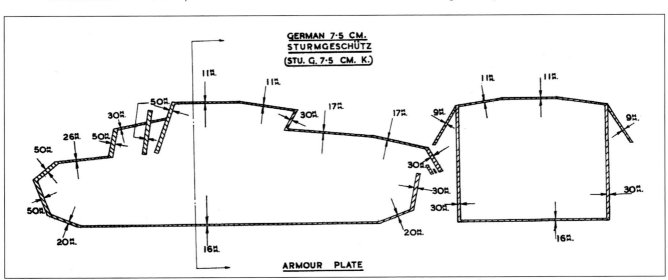

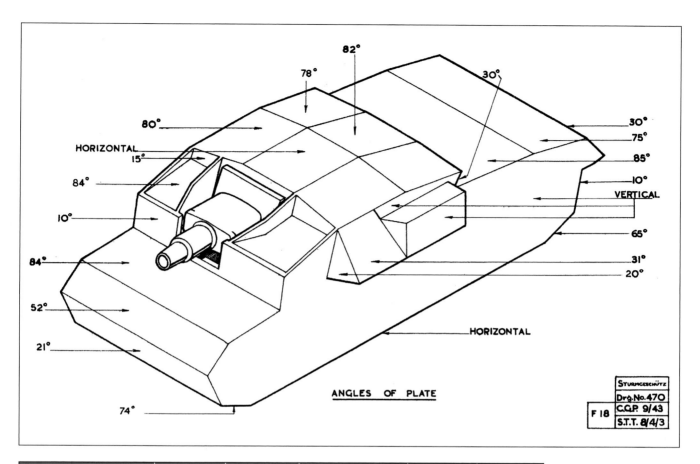

ANGLES OF PLATE

| STURMGESCHÜTZ |
| Drg.No.470 |
| C.G.P. 9/43 |
| S.T.T. 8/4/3 |

F 18

ABOVE Armour plate angles, general perspective view.

Position of armour plate	Thickness (mm)	Angle °	Position of armour plate	Thickness (mm)	Angle °
Top of fighting compartment	11	80° sides 90° centre	Side of fighting compartment	30	0°
Rear of fighting compartment	11	78° sides 82° centre	Side hull plate	30	0°
Sides of fighting compartment	30	30°	Top front plate	30	84°
Front of superstructure	50	15°	Top rear plate	17	85°
Gun mantlet	50	15°	Top engine cover plate	17	75°
Front vertical plate	50	10°	Observation cover plate	50	
Front glacis plate	26	84°	Belly plate front	20	74°
Front nose plate	50	52°	Belly plate middle	16	90°

Armour hardness

The effectiveness of the armour on the assault gun was not just a consequence of either its thickness or of the angle at which it was mounted. It also stemmed from the quality – that is, the hardness of the armour actually employed. This was assessed by the British Army team evaluating the assault gun by employment of the Poldi method and measured on the Brinell scale. The Poldi method used an indenter. This was a small body with a hard tip, which functioned as a probe that was directed against the armour of the Sturmgeschütz. The motion of the probe is the measure of its kinetic energy, which is then converted into a chosen scale of conventional hardness. In this case, that employed was the Brinell scale where the higher the Brinell number the greater the hardness.

Results of the Poldi tests on parts of the StuG III armour	
Position of armour plate	Brinell number
Superstructure top front	388
Turret side	336
Gun mantlet	501
Gun recuperator front cover plate	585
Front vertical plate	339
Front upper nose plate	524–572
Front lower nose plate	495–519
Side hull plate	360
Tail plate (upper)	548

BELOW The torsion bar suspension of the StuG III is illustrated in this graphic. Although the number of torsion bars remained the same throughout the type's career, the thicknesses of a number changed (see text). The drive sprockets and idler wheels are those of the first variant of the StuG III – the Ausf A.

Suspension

All models of the Sturmgeschütz from A through to G employed a torsion bar suspension. This is hardly surprising as the hull and suspension were all based upon different variants of the Panzer III chassis modified for use on the assault gun over the course of the former's production life. Although torsion bar systems are extremely common on modern tanks, when first introduced in the mid- to late 1930s, they were regarded as a modern innovation. Having its origins in the development work of a Czech engineer by the name of Hans Ledwinka who worked for Tatra, this company was taken over and employed by the Germans following the occupation of that country in 1939. Although the Panzer IV did not employ this type of suspension, it was used on the Panzer III, Panther, Tiger I and Tiger II and post-war on the

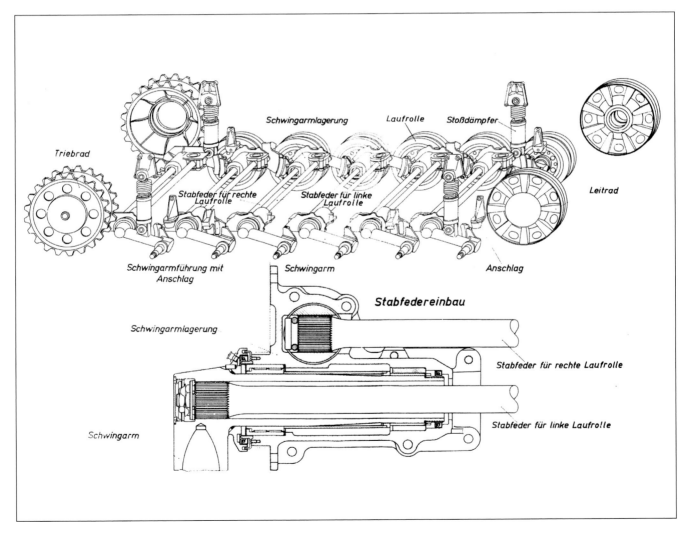

Leopard I and Leopard II Main Battle Tanks. A generic and very succinct explanation of how a torsion bar system works is found in the *Haynes Panzer III Manual* and is reproduced here:

'When a roadwheel encounters uneven ground it needs to move up and down, and as much as possible the forces transmitted to it should be prevented from being transmitted in turn to the hull and crew. Therefore the suspension has two requirements: to absorb the shock by some form of spring, and then to damp the oscillations quickly to return the spring back to its resting state, otherwise the suspension will cause the vehicle to bounce. A torsion bar does this by using a long bar of treated steel that runs transversely across the bottom of the vehicle hull. It is fixed at the end opposite the wheel it works with. The wheel axle is fitted to the bar, such that when moving up and down the bar itself twists in response to the motion of the wheel. Resistance to the twisting force provides the damping. The system is simple with few external components, but does take up some of the scarce internal space at the bottom of the hull, and can be time consuming to change if a torsion bar breaks or cracks.'

It is surprising that the designers chose from the outset to employ torsion bars of differing thicknesses for the Sturmgeschütz. This naturally caused unnecessary complications with logistics when utilisation of torsion bars of the same thickness would have made life a lot easier. It certainly would have impacted on production costs. Thus in the Ausf A through to the final example of the Ausf E the thicknesses of the six torsion bars per roadwheel, moving from front to back, were as follows:

O	O	O	O	O	O
55mm	52mm	44mm	44mm	52mm	55mm

In February 1942 it had become apparent that the thicknesses of the torsion bars were no longer adequate to support a hull that had become heavier by virtue of increases in the thickness of the armour being carried and, in the move in the F/8, to a new, longer and heavier main gun. Therefore, the thicknesses of the torsion bars were increased to accommodate this as follows:

O	O	O	O	O	O
55mm	55mm	55mm	52mm	52mm	52mm

Although these thicknesses obtained to the end of the war they nonetheless still continued to fail as the weight of the StuG increased; e.g. Ausf A – 19.6 tons when compared to the StuG at 24 tons.

In some photographs spare torsion bars can be seen attached to the lower hull between the top and bottom track runs.

Running gear

The **drive sprockets** of the running gear fitted to the models A–E exhibited changes in appearance that constituted one of the most obvious distinguishing features.

- **Ausf A:** The drive sprocket was designed for a 38cm track and had eight equidistant positioned holes. A central hex screw secured the hub cap on the sprocket.
- **Ausf B**: On those Ausf Bs built by Alkett between June and December 1940 the same eight-holed drive sprocket was fitted for a 38cm track. Surviving machines were fitted with spacer rings to permit the drive sprocket to take the slightly wider 40cm track introduced in December 1940.
- In December 1940, Alkett introduced a new drive sprocket on the Ausf B with six spokes. This was manufactured from the outset to take a wider 40cm track. This same sprocket would be employed by Alkett on all Sturmgeschützen built by the company through to March 1944 and were thus fitted to all remaining Ausf B and later Ausf C, Ausf D and Ausf E.

In the same fashion that the changes in the drive sprockets provide a recognition feature, the rear **idler wheels** do the same, albeit there are only two variants.

- **Ausf A**: A complex design comprising a double disc roller with 8 equidistant reinforcing ribs between which were 8 oval-shaped holes. This design continued to be employed through to the Ausf B manufactured by Alkett in March 1941.

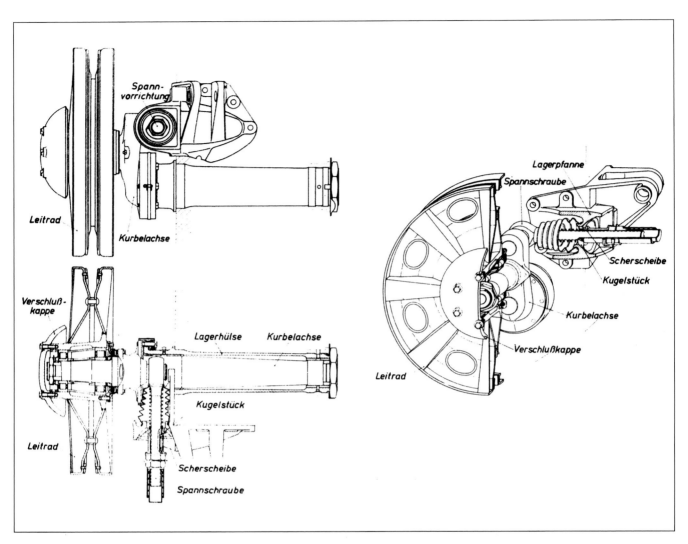

Spann-vorrichtung

Leitrad

Kurbelachse

Verschluß-kappe

Leitrad

Lagerhülse   Kurbelachse

Kugelstück

Scherscheibe

Spannschraube

Lagerpfanne

Spannschraube

Scherscheibe

Kugelstück

Kurbelachse

Verschlußkappe

Leitrad

Thereafter, Alkett introduced a new welded steel-rimmed idler wheel in March 1941. This was employed on all StuGs built by the company thereafter through to the end of the conflict.

Roadwheels

Two types of roadwheels were employed on all models of the Sturmgeschütz.

■ On the Ausf A built by Daimler-Benz between January and May 1940 the roadwheels were narrow to run on the 38cm track. These roadwheels measured 520 x 95 – 397. The rubber tyres were solid and sourced from a number of producers, primarily by the Continental Company.

■ From June 1940 – that is, from the manufacture of the second production of Ausf As through to the end of May/June

1944 – the roadwheels were enlarged to fit the wider 40cm track and were sized to 520 x 95 – 397/398. The massive expansion of StuG III production from 1943 onwards had seen other companies other than just Continental brought in to produce the rubber tyres. These included Fulda, DEKA, Vorwerk, Semperit, Metzeler and Dunlop.

Return rollers

■ The three return rollers on the Ausf A were distinguished by being placed equidistant from one another. This obtained through to the second production batch of the Ausf A in September 1940.

■ With the introduction of the Ausf B on the Alkett production line in June 1940 the relationship of the return rollers was changed, such that there now appeared an unequal gap between the three, with a larger one between one and two than between two and three. This arrangement continued through to war's end.

■ All short-barrelled StuGs employed rubber tyres on the three return rollers.

Tracks

It is hardly surprising that over the course of its production life the tracks of the Sturmgeschütz exhibited many changes/modifications as a consequence of the need to respond to the conditions experienced in combat. This was especially so as the bulk of all StuGs were employed in Russia where the extreme climatic conditions made strenuous demands of all German armoured vehicles.

Three types of track were employed on StuG models A–E. These cover those models built by Alkett. It should be noted that the manner in which the width of a tank track was recorded

included the track pins. This led to them being declared as 2cm wider than they really were, e.g. the 38cm track was in actuality 36cm wide.

■ Track width of all Ausf As – including the second batch – was of 38cm width. The track horn at the centre was open. Only a single side-bar.

■ Introduction of the Ausf B in mid-1940 saw the track width increased to 40cm. Each had two grooves and an open track horn. Single side-bar.

■ In March 1941 Alkett changed the track. It retained the same 40cm width and open track horn but was now equipped with a double side-bar to enable fitting of hammer-type cleats or a snow chevron – with both offering greater traction and grip for different weather conditions. First fitted to the Ausf C and continued being fitted to the war's end.

INVESTIGATING TRACK FAILURE ON THE STUG AUSF D

In its report on the Sturmgeschütz Ausf D the British Army evaluation team noted an 'interesting failure of the tracks . . . that a number of the plates having fractured at the base of the track horn. The failure is common to both tracks and is also not confined to those emanating from one foundry, since the affected plates bear the markings of two manufacturers. A spare track plate stowed on the vehicle, which had this defect, has been repaired by welding. There are 50 defective plates in the offside track and 26 on the nearside.'

It further stated that samples of these defective plates were submitted to Messrs Birmingham Electric Furnaces Ltd for examination and their report is quoted below.

Examination of defective PzKpfw III track links

'Failure had occurred on both links by cracking at the point where the horn joins the body of the link on the four-lug side.

'One of the links was cut up, and microsection prepared of the metal at this point. This showed the material to be austenitic manganese steel of normal structure and grain size and more homogeneous than the sample link of this type examined some time ago; the amount of martensite in the surface layers was not more than would be expected to result from work hardening under service conditions.

'Hardness of the body of the metal was 215–225 VPN, which is normal. The section showed numerous cracks at the point of failure, starting from the upper side of the link and spreading inwards; the cracks were mainly intergranular but a piece of metal from near this point showed no sign of abnormal intergranular weakness where fractured.

'When cutting up this link, shrinkage cavities were found at some points, notably where the centre lug joins the body of the casting on the three-lug side, but there were no signs of marked unsoundness at the point where cracking occurred and no evidence that this was a primary cause of weakness.

'Conclusions drawn that the material of these links is of normal structure and properties, but that the manganese steel, of normal structure and properties, but that the thickness of the metal at the point of failure is insufficient to withstand the transverse bending stresses encountered in service, with the result that failure has occurred by fatigue cracking.'

It is worth noting that the tracks were stamped with the markings of the foundries from which they originated and bore the following respective markings:

(1) 2034 eyc;
(2) ccq 2079 bwo 1941.

Hull interior – StuG Ausf D

Interior layout

The interior of the armoured hull was divided into two by a firewall that separated the engine compartment from the fighting compartment. The firewall was provided with a door so that the crew could gain access to the engine compartment, but this was limited.

Fitted above the six torsion bars that spanned the lower hull of the StuG were a number of anti-skid plates. These were removable in the event that access was needed to get to the torsion bars, should one or more need to be replaced because of damage.

Facing forward in the front of the fighting compartment, the driver's position was to the left of the transmission, which was placed in the centre. The driveshaft from the engine in the rear section was connected to the clutch on the transmission. This driveshaft ran back to the firewall encased in a tunnel, along the floor of the fighting compartment. In front of the transmission, connecting bevel gears were linked to the steering gears. Two more connectors were attached both to the drive brakes located on the lower left and right of the forward hull and also the final drives connected to the drive sprockets. This general layout can be seen in the profile and plan view of the basic interior silhouette view of the StuG.

RIGHT Engine and drive train arrangement. Top image: the layout inside the hull of the Maybach engine (in the rear), the drive shaft leading from the engine to the transmission. In the plan view below, the same can be seen with the position of the cooling fans for the engine and the way power was transmitted via the transmission shaft to the drive shafts linking through to the drive sprockets.

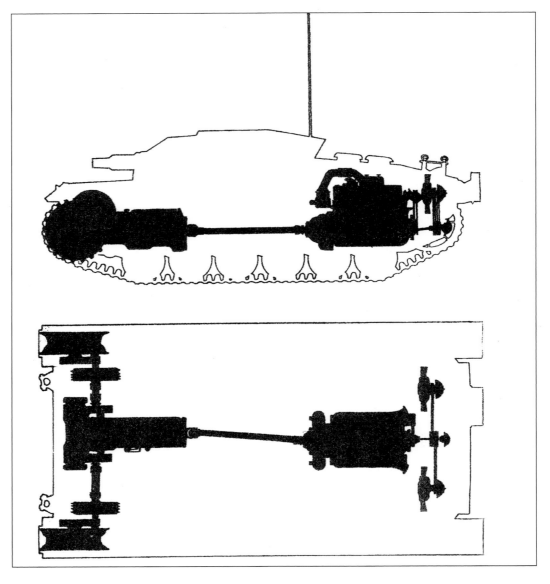

From his seat the driver controlled the StuG by means of two steering levers – one for each track. The steering was hydraulically operated as on the PzKpfw III Ausf F with an epicyclic clutch, as were the brakes. However, no air intake cowls were fitted in the nose plate to aid brake cooling. The driver had access to seven gears, all of which were manual. There were six forward gears and one reverse. The gear lever was positioned on his right as was the starter carburettor control and the steering tensioning lever. The instrument panel was also to the driver's right and mounted above the transmission. From his seating position the driver's feet would extend over the left drive shaft to access the accelerator, clutch and brake pedals.

Armament

As has already been mentioned the production of the Sturmgeschütz III falls naturally into two phases with these being determined by the nature of the armament they are mounting. Until March 1942, when the first long-barrelled StuK

(Sturmkanone) 40 75mm L/43 guns started being mounted on the Ausf F, all preceding StuGs had been equipped with the short 75mm StuK 37 L/24. The last of these E models left the Alkett factory in January 1942. This section addresses those StuGs carrying the

ABOVE This is the driver's position in the front lower left-hand side of the StuG's fighting compartment (with the driver). In front of him are the two steering columns for controlling the left and right tracks.

LEFT In this view the external visor is closed and the two telescopes used by the driver are folded down. On the bottom left can be seen the speaking tube used by the driver to speak to the vehicle commander and vice versa. On later models of StuG the crew communicated by intercom.

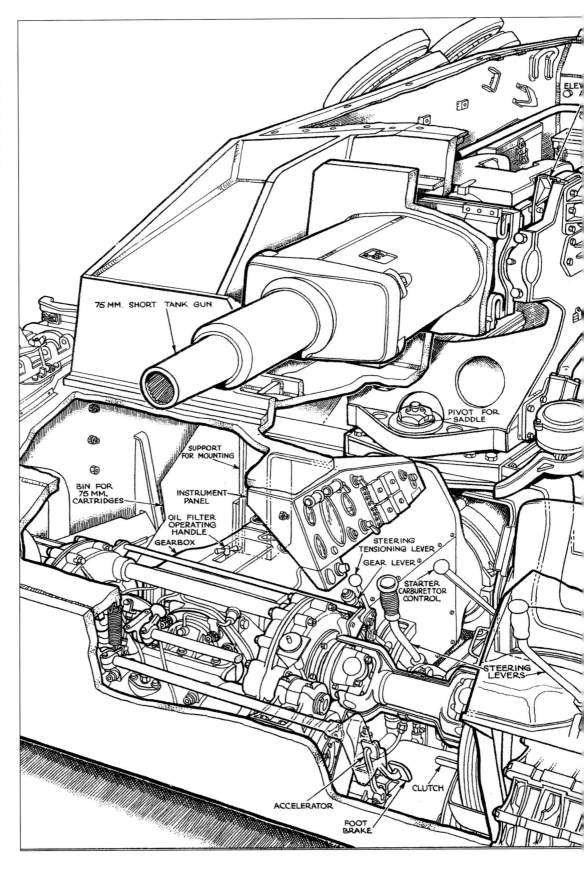

RIGHT A detailed cutaway of the interior of a StuG III Ausf D. Much of the text in this chapter should be read in conjunction with this drawing. The inset provides a detailed image of the mounting carriage for the 75mm L/24 main gun.

75 MM. SHORT TANK GUN

PIVOT FOR SADDLE

SUPPORT FOR MOUNTING

BIN FOR 75 MM. CARTRIDGES

INSTRUMENT PANEL

OIL FILTER OPERATING HANDLE

GEARBOX

STEERING TENSIONING LEVER

GEAR LEVER

STARTER CARBURETTOR CONTROL

STEERING LEVERS

ACCELERATOR

FOOT BRAKE

CLUTCH

ELEV

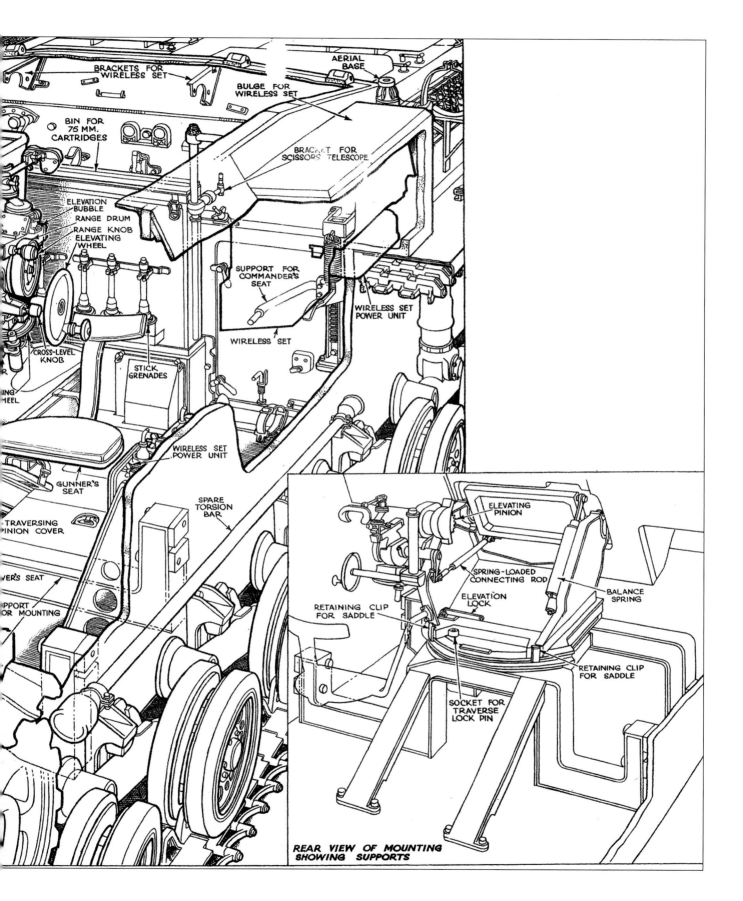

BRACKETS FOR
WIRELESS SET

AERIAL
BASE

BULGE FOR
WIRELESS SET

BIN FOR
75 MM.
CARTRIDGES

BRACKET FOR
SCISSORS TELESCOPE

ELEVATION
BUBBLE
RANGE DRUM
RANGE KNOB
ELEVATING
WHEEL

SUPPORT FOR
COMMANDER'S
SEAT

WIRELESS SET
POWER UNIT

CROSS-LEVEL
KNOB

STICK
GRENADES

WIRELESS SET

WIRELESS SET
POWER UNIT

GUNNER'S
SEAT

SPARE
TORSION
BAR

TRAVERSING
PINION COVER

ELEVATING
PINION

ER'S SEAT

SPRING-LOADED
CONNECTING ROD

BALANCE
SPRING

PORT
OR MOUNTING

ELEVATION
LOCK

RETAINING CLIP
FOR SADDLE

RETAINING CLIP
FOR SADDLE

SOCKET FOR
TRAVERSE
LOCK PIN

REAR VIEW OF MOUNTING
SHOWING SUPPORTS

short-barrelled weapon with coverage of those mounting the longer-barrelled weapon being covered separately.

There was no change in the specification of the 75mm StuK 37 L/24 main gun during the production life of the Ausf A–E:

- The reason why the StuG carrying this weapon was sometimes called the '*Stummel*' (German for stump or cigar/cigarette butt) by its crews was due to its short gun barrel, that is just 1,766.5mm in length and was essentially the same as that fitted on the Panzer IV Ausf A–F1.
- It was equipped with a monobloc barrel with detachable breech ring. It had a semi-automatic vertical sliding wedge breech block operated by separate clock springs

MARKINGS FOUND ON THE BREECH AND BARREL

The breech ring was inscribed thus:
1941. R.459.csf.Bs.Sg 60504
R1.2194. Rhm.394.F1.236.csf
WaA.337. Vr.F1.203 csf

The breech block was inscribed thus:
R.459. Sg. 60066. R1. 1037. Rh 206. F1. 209. Csf.

The barrel was inscribed thus:
Vr. Sg 5324. R1 148. Rh.206 F1. 203. Csf.

for opening and closing. It employed electric primer firing.

- The weapon had a maximum range of 6,000m.
- Weight of the weapon was 490kg (1,080lb).
- The weapon had a limited degree of movement. It could be traversed through 24° and had an elevation arc from -10 to +20°.

Captured documents indicated that the gun had fired at least 236 rounds.

The report describes the cradle as being similar to that used by the PzKpfw IV Model A to E and is of a welded construction. The left-hand gun lug is provided with bronze shoes and runs in an anti-rotation guide inside the left side plate of the cradle. The SA gear is the same as on the PzKpfw IV Models B to E. To render the weapon ineffective in the event of it needing to be abandoned, the cam carrier was removed from its slide on the cradle side plate, after pulling out the plunger.

The deflector guard was bolted in position and carried a small-capacity empty cartridge bag, with a flap at the rear for removal of empty cartridge cases.

The recoil system

This comprised a hydraulic buffer on the right and a hydro-pneumatic recuperator on the left. Both are similar to those employed on the PzKpfw IV Ausf B to E, except that the recuperator follows that of the PzKpfw III and later PzKpfw IV in having the charging hole and charging valve drilled vertically instead of axially.

There is a spring loaded hydraulic reservoir for the buffer, with a safety switch, slung in the usual place. However, the construction of the pedestal on which the mounting stands makes the filling plug inaccessible. To overcome this a pipe is taken from the filling hole to a filling box on the outside of the left cradle side plate. The non-return valve is also incorporated in this box.

The piston rods are nutted to lugs formed on either side of the breech ring. A recoil indicator is provided inside the left cradle side plate and is graduated from 380 to 470mm with the *Feuerpause* (Stop) at 455mm. The buffer reservoir appears to be empty, but the system seems otherwise serviceable.

Main gun mounting

It was observed that the gun mounting in the StuG is similar to that employed on the eight-wheeled, schwere Panzerspähwagen 233, a number of which were captured by the Allies in Tunisia in the first half of 1943. This carried the same 75mm StuK 37 L/24 as the StuG III. It comprised a heavy rectangular frame carrying the trunnions, the mantlet and cradle. This permitted the main armament to be raised to a maximum elevation of 20° and a maximum depression of 11°.

The mantlet is secured to the front of the mounting by four U-shaped brackets, which appear to have been designed to give a certain amount of spring. A small cover plate is provided on top of the mantlet for access to the plug and valve on the front of the recuperator. There was no attempt to provide splash protection in order to keep out rain/dust. However, a canvas joint cover was provided.

Firing gear

This is in the form of a standard electric primer system operated by a trigger on the traversing wheel. Current is provided from the vehicle battery (12V) or from an emergency battery (9V or 4½V).

Balance

The weight of the mantlet makes the mounting muzzle heavy (and it became even more so with the introduction of the 7mm L/43 and L/48 weapons). This is balanced by a compression spring carried in a cylinder connected between the mounting frame and saddle on the right-hand side. There are no counter-weights.

BELOW The superstructure has been lifted off the hull to expose the fighting compartment of the StuG. The body of the 75mm main gun and its breech occupies most of the length of the compartment. Clearly seen is the control wheel for elevating the gun.

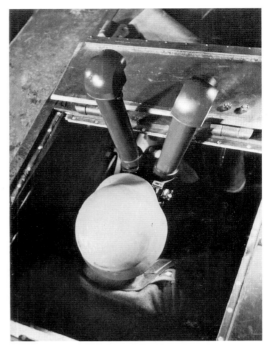

ABOVE, ABOVE RIGHT AND BELOW The gunner is adjusting his Sfl-ZF
1 periscope gunsight, which was located on the left-hand side of the gun
mounting. The commander, who is wearing his steel helmet, is employing his
Scherenfernrohr – his scissors-type periscope to view targets ahead. Both
scopes can be seen deployed in this image showing how the StuG would
have looked in combat. In the later 'G' model of the StuG III the scissors
periscope could be raised through a small hatch, which allowed him to view
the exterior even when closed down.

Elevating gear

That provided is of a sector and pinion type.
It is operated by a 4in radius handwheel on a
transverse shaft though two bevel wheels, and
a worm and wormwheel. Twenty turns of the
handwheel are required to cover the full arc
of 31°.

Traversing gear

This also comprised a sector and pinion type.
The sector is bolted to the pedestal and the
pinion is driven by a handwheel on a vertical
axis through two sets of bevel gears, two
universal joints, a third set of bevel gears, and a
worm and wormwheel.

The arc of traverse = 25° – viz 12½° to the
right and left. Thirteen turns of the handwheel
were required to cover the full arc of 25°.

Saddle

The saddle is of a welded construction and
carries the following:

- Trunnion bearings
- Balance gear anchorage
- Gunner's seat
- Elevation travelling lock stay
- Traverse lock
- Brackets for elevating, traversing and
  sighting gear.

Pedestal

This was of a built-up welded construction, supported astride the propeller shaft on four legs and provided with two buttresses at the rear. It is so located that the axis of the bore is offset 4½in to the right.

Sighting gear

Unlike that equipping the Panzer IV, which was specifically designed for employment in tanks, the sighting gear utilised by the StuG was of an artillery type. The sight bracket was mounted on its own trunnions and linked by drop arms and a connecting rod. The connecting rod was spring-loaded and would compress if the sight bracket fouled the hull of the vehicle. Such a possibility occurred if the sight was set for long range without the gun being elevated.

A more detailed coverage of the sighting processes is provided here:

1) **Angle of sight** with bubble:
   From 100 to 500 mils in units – 300 mils represents zero angle of sight.
2) **Tangent elevation and range** engraved on a range drum.
   The scales on the drum are as follows:
   a) **TE** – 0 to 360 mils graduated in twos.
   b) **Range – 75mm Sprgr. KwK (Gr.34)**
      0 to 3,000m graduated in 100s.
      3,000 to 6,000m in 50s.
   c) **Range – for KwK.K.Gr.rot. Pz**
      0 to 1,500 graduated in 100s.
   The zeroes are not displaced for jump.
3) **Cross levelling with bubble**
   There is no scale. The actual sight is a dial sight (but in the view of the British evaluating officers it was deficient). This sight, when employed, projected through a hatch in the roof. In the Ausf D there was no armoured flap, instead the space was covered by a canvas flap when not in use. The gunner was provided with a browpad when employing the sight. Provision was made for illuminating the graticule in the event of poor visibility and darkness.

Observation of fire

The commander of the StuG is provided with a swinging bracket which supports the 'SF.14Z' scissors telescope, which projects through his hatch when in action. When not in use the bracket folds down and the binoculars are strapped to the left wall of the fighting compartment.

It was an accepted fact within the Wehrmacht that the quality of the sights fitted to the StuG were superior – and this would apply to all models between 1940 and 1945 – when compared to panzers. They were more powerful, permitting a greater magnification and those for the gunner were added to by the binocular sight that was also available to the commander. The StuG in consequence was equipped with a superior range-finding capacity. It was this factor that, more than any other, explains the ability of the StuG to defeat Russian tanks, even though the 75mm L/48 weapon was the same as that fitted to the Panzer IVG onward. This was further accentuated by the bracketing method used by StuG crews who belonged in the main to the artillery. To this was also allied the superior training received by German StuG and panzer crews when compared to their Russian opponents.

Ammunition

Four types of ammunition (all illustrated below) could be fired by the '*Stummel*'.

a) **75mm K.Gr.rot Pz** – with a velocity of 385m/sec. This was a capped armour-piercing shell with high-explosive filler.
b) **75mm Gr.34** – with velocity of 420m/sec. This was a high-explosive shell.
c) **75mm Gr.38 H1** – with a velocity of 450m/sec. This was a high-explosive anti-tank round used to take on and defeat enemy armour.
d) **75mm Nebel-Gr** – smoke shell.
e) **75mm Gr Patr 38** – this was a shaped charge round (Hohlladungsgeschosse) developed to give the L/24 main gun a more effective anti-tank capability. It was introduced in January 1942.

Stowage of the ammunition

The ammunition boxes of the StuG Ausf D were sized to carry 44 rounds of ammunition in varying combinations of those listed above. However, crews often carried extra

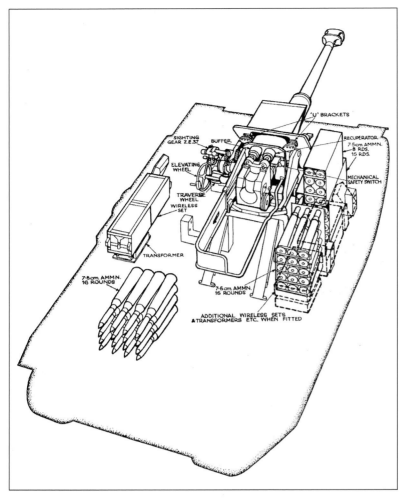

The boxes are of sheet metal with hinged lids and quick release clips. They are each provided with three diaphragms in which the rounds are stowed nose downwards. They are clearly designed as part of the vehicle. Nonetheless, it was noted by the British evaluation team that 'one curious feature is that the lowest diaphragm is provided with a spring-loaded plastic ring to position the nose of each shell, but in all cases the spring operates so as to press the ring away from the shell instead of against it. In other words it seems to serve no useful purpose.'

Auxiliary weapons

There is stowage for 12 stick grenades. These were held in clips in a row mounted on the front of the ammunition box attached to the engine bulkhead. The Ausf D was the first StuG to be outfitted with an MG34. This was stowed when not in use, standing upright, in the right rear corner of the fighting compartment behind the loader.

To the right rear of the hull there was an armoured ejector rack that carried five smoke candles. A machine carbine (MP38/40) and ammunition were also normally stowed on the rear wall. (However, on this particular example these were removed to generate space for a larger wireless set that was fitted.)

Electrical equipment

The hull electrical equipment arrangements of this vehicle are identical to that of the PzKpfw III. Two 12V accumulators in the engine compartment give 24V for starting and 12V for lighting etc., the changeover to the series connection of the batteries being carried out by a solenoid switch operated by the starter button. Charging is by a 12V generator with voltage regulation.

The external lighting consists of two headlamps in blastproof cases, two sidelights and a normal tail stoplight. The usual German night march lighting system is also fitted.

Internal lighting is confined to one festoon lamp on the fighting compartment's roof and two festoon lamps on the driver's panel.

Crew

The StuG had a crew of four. The commander, gunner and driver were (looking forward from the rear) all seated on the left side of the vehicle

ABOVE The official way of storing ammunition in the StuG III Ausf G. Some 54 rounds could be carried in this fashion as the StuH carried 36 rounds. However, tank crews loaded more ammunition often by taking out the containers in which the rounds were stored. In some cases StuGs were known to carry up to 96 rounds into action with every bit of space in the fighting compartment taken up for storing ammunition.

ammunition that was stored in spaces in the hull. Officially stowed ammunition was stored as follows:

No of rounds

Fixed box for: 4)	To the right of the gun
Fixed box for: 3)	mounting aperture.
Loose box for: 3)	Below mounting
Loose box for: 3)	aperture on
Loose box for: 2)	the right of the
Loose box for: 2)	gearbox
Fixed box for: 5)	
Fixed box for: 5)	On right of pedestal
Fixed box for: 5)	
Detachable box for: 12)	In rear of fighting
	compartment.

Total number of rounds: 44

RIGHT The driver's viewing plate was actually made of a synthetic glass and in combat the armoured visor could be lowered to protect it from combat damage, as can be seen in the second image below. Above the visor are the two telescopes employed by the driver. In the third image the driver's visor is open and the dual telescopes are ready for use. On the left of the picture can be seen a small visor in the hull side that gave the driver a limited perspective on what was happening on the flank. It was also armoured and could be closed.

and to the left of the transmission shaft. The loader was seated in the right corner of the hull.

The fighting chamber, which contained all but the driver, had the following internal dimensions:

Headroom (max):	4ft 8in
Width:	6ft 1in
Length (approx):	5ft 1in

The commander had a spring-loaded rising seat, which was locked by a foot pedal. This enabled him to look out over the roof or to observe from under cover employing the 14Z (SF 14Z) 10 x magnification scissors periscope with a 5° angle of view.

The gunner's seat was attached to the saddle. Sighting for the gunner was provided by a Panoramic Telescope 32 (Rbl.F.32) with a 4 x magnification and a 10° angle of view.

No seat was provided for the loader.

The driver's seat was the same as that found on the PzKpfw IV. He was provided with a normal elongated laminated glass block and shutter. In addition the driver employed an episcope formed by two KFF2 periscopic telescopes, which had no magnification with a 65° angle of view. (It was noted by the British evaluation team that 'the carrier for these is deficient, but it must differ from the normal type since there is no room on the right to slide it away when not in use. Presumably, the carrier is pivoted and swings away to the left.) On the driver's left only was a fixed slit backed by a 50mm laminated glass block.

Access to the driver's compartment was normally made through the gunner's hatch, but he could also exit through the steering brake inspection flaps in the glacis plate. Each of

LEFT The StuG commander had oversight of the radio, it being fitted on the left of his position. Comprising a FuG 15 radio it was equipped with a UHF receiver and a transformer mounted below the radio set. On the left the speaking tube is also used to snag the commander's headphones.

these flaps comprises two doors of equal size, hinged to the sides.

Communications equipment

By the time of Operation 'Barbarossa' in June 1941, all StuGs from Ausf A to D had been equipped with two radios. The first of these was the FuG 16 10W S 'h' shortwave transmitter as well as a FuG 15 UHF E 'h' ultra-high frequency receiver. It was this latter wireless that permitted full radio contact between vehicles in the battery. The appearance of the Ausf E allowed for the fitting of an extra FuG 15 inside a platoon and a battery leader's vehicle.

Engine compartment

The engine compartment was separated from that of the fighting compartment by a firewall. This was sited directly beneath where the rear of the superstructure met the engine deck. A small door was provided in the firewall to allow one of the crew access to the engine compartment.

Whereas the 4 Serie ZW chassis/PzKpfw III Ausf E and thus the StuG Ausf A employed the Maybach 120TR engine, with the introduction of the StuG Ausf B, all assault guns built thereafter through to the end of Ausf G production in 1945 utilised the later Maybach HL120 TRM. It is this engine that is the subject of the following description and thus covers all models from the Ausf B through to the G.

The Maybach HL120 TRM was a V-12, water-cooled, four-stroke engine which generated 296bhp at 3,000rpm. This was sited to the rear of the hull with its radiators and cooling fans, being mounted on both sides of the engine. Two Solex downdraught duplex petrol carburettors fed the engine from a single fuel tank, which was located on the right side of the engine. This tank held 310 litres. The air cleaners were of a four-oil bath-type.

A drive shaft connected the engine to the transmission (see diagram) with the shaft running

---

MANUFACTURER'S MARKINGS

On plate on driver's instrument panel:
- ■ Gp. SFL. fürStu. G. 7.5 cm. K.
- ■ Sd.Kfz 142 Ausf.
- ■ Fahrgest Nr: 90683 csg

On plate on engine:
- ■ NORDEUTSCHE – MOTORENBAU G.m.b.H.
- ■ Motortyp: HL. 120TRM
- ■ Leistung: 300 P.S.
- ■ Motor No: 541379

On carburettors:
- ■ 1) SOLEX DRP Deutsche Vergasser Gesellech
       40 JFF 2. 2 K 264
- ■ 2) SOLEX DRP Deutsche Vergasser Gesellech
       40 JFF 2. 2 K 164

On radiators:
- ■ JHANS WINDHOFF–BERLIN–SCHONENBURG
- ■ N/Side: Kuhl Nr: 90572
       Com Nr: 44335
       Lfd N: 23   7   41
       4419: L.81
- ■ O/side: OKuhl Nr: 90373
       Com No: 44838
       Lfd Nr: 24. 41
       4423 R 75

BELOW The Maybach HL120 TRM petrol engine was utilised by all StuG variants except for the Ausf A, which employed the HL120 TR, as well as powering the Panzer III and Panzer IV (the Ausf J employed the HL120 TRM 112). It was a reliable engine that still had sufficient capacity to power the StuG, even as its weight grew in the war years.

along the length of the floor of the fighting compartment within a tunnel. This connected the engine to the clutch, which was mounted on the transmission that was positioned in the front and centre of the compartment to the right of the driver's position. In front of the transmission were located the connecting bevel gears that were fixed to the steering gears. Two connectors led to the brakes and also the final drives on either side of the transmission.

Performance of the StuG Ausf D	
Max speed	25mph (approx)
Step	2ft 0in
Trench	8ft 6in
Fording	2ft 9in
Gradient	27°
Radius of action – road	105 miles
cross-country	56 miles
Fuel consumption – road	1.5mpg
cross-country	0.8mpg

RIGHT With the fighting compartment and the engine deck removed it is possible to see where the former ends and the latter begins. Removal of the engine deck allowed easy access to the powerplant and, providing it was not in need of extensive repair work in which case the whole engine would be returned to the factory in Germany to be repaired, the Workstatt unit would deal with most other problems.

Chapter Five

Anatomy of the StuG III Ausf F, F/8 and Ausf G

In this chapter the anatomy of the long-barrelled StuG III Ausf F, F/8 and G is examined. The first two of these variants carrying this new weapon used much the same chassis and body as the Ausf E. In December 1942 the introduction of the modified Ausf G, and the production of the Sturmhaubitze in March 1943, saw the StuG display the features (both internal and external) that it would retain until April 1945.

OPPOSITE Rearming on the Steppe in mid-winter 1942–43. This F/8 that belongs to StuGAbt 901 is being rearmed by a surviving SdKfz 252, very few of which were still operating by this time.

Structurally the new model Ausf F was identical to that of the previous Ausf E, apart from raising the frontal armour from 50mm to 80mm and the addition of a new roof ventilator to extract exhaust fumes from the fighting compartment after the main armament had been fired. The change to the armament is detailed in the section on the same for the Ausf F/8.

Changes to the hull on the F/8

Although the StuG III F/8 was preceded by seven earlier series of assault guns, the hulls employed had been basically the same. In the case of this variant, the eighth of the series, the F/8 evidenced significant changes reflecting the employment of an 8/ZW chassis based on the Panzer III Ausf L through to Ausf M. In consequence of the need to increase output of the StuG, Alkett ceased production of the Panzer III in September 1942 with the hulls of that tank being employed, albeit modified, for the StuG Ausf F/8. Indeed, some 80% of all Ausf F/8s were constructed directly on the Panzer III chassis.

It was the growing preference being expressed for the StuG over that of the Panzer III that led Alkett to discontinue production of the latter and employ its hull on the StuG F/8.

The StuG thus inherited the distinctive features of the late Panzer III hull. Most noticeable was an extension forward of the upper hull sidewalls to incorporate two front towing holes to act as towing brackets. Shackles could be attached to these brackets. The engine decking was also modified by being extended further to the rear and the design of the air-louvres was improved to permit more effective ventilation to the engine compartment. The increase in the rear hull armour is covered in the section on 'armour'.

Changes to the armour on the Ausf F

In the case of the new additional armour, an extra 30mm-thick slab of armour was welded on to the already extant 50mm frontal hull armour, as built, to yield a thickness of 80mm. This change had been mandated on 20 June

1942 by Target Order No 8. This required that all StuGs equipped with the longer 75mm StuK 40 were to be so equipped when built. As the StuG III Ausf F had first left the production line at Alkett in March 1942, those built through to June retained the 50mm frontal armour. The first StuGs produced evidencing this upgrading of their frontal armour emerged in June 1942, and this was to continue through to July with 60 having been manufactured with the 80mm frontal armour and none with just 50mm. Of note, is that on the final 11 Ausf Fs to leave the production line in June 1942, additional 30mm armour plates were also welded to the 50mm plates on the upper and lower nose plates of the hull – that is, above and below the frontal armour already increased – and also to the forward 50mm baseplates of the superstructure.

At the beginning of August 1942, the angle of the armoured plates above the driver and also on the other side of the opening for the main gun was changed. When viewed from the front the StuG now presented an unbroken appearance from the front plate to beginning of the superstructure roof. This enhanced the protection of the front of the assault gun, rendering it less vulnerable to penetration by enemy fire. It is worth noting, that for those crews not operating StuG III Ausf Fs equipped with this updated armour protection on either side of the gun aperture, a substitute expedient – albeit not as effective – was the addition of a layer of concrete spread to effect the same profile. This was a field modification and not one officially sanctioned as it was deemed to be ineffective. Nonetheless, it certainly had a positive psychological value for the StuG crews as this feature continued to be seen on many StuGs through to the end of the conflict.

In the case of the StuG III F/8, which was produced by Alkett from September 1942, the primary distinguishing feature of this variant was that the extra 30mm armour plate added to the front of the hull was in contradistinction to that mounted on the preceding model, bolted on and not welded.

Armament

It was the introduction of the 75mm StuK 40 L/43 on to the remaining 366 contracted

ABOVE This StuG III Ausf F supports infantry in the foothills of the Caucasus Mountains in the summer of 1942.

StuG III Ausf Es that saw the introduction of the new designation of the Ausf F. As the only difference between the 75mm StuK 40 L/43 of the Ausf F/8 and the 75 mm StuK 40 L/48 was the latter's slightly longer barrel – with identical ammunition being employed on both weapons – it is advantageous to address both weapons together. For this reason the armament of the F/8 will be covered within that of the L/48 weapon of the StuG Ausf G.

Anatomy of the StuG III Ausf G SdKfz Nr 142/1

In December 1942, Alkett introduced the first real substantive change in the appearance of the Sturmgeschütz since the Ausf A in 1940. All the previous variant updates had been improvements on that initial model. The Ausf G, which was to remain in production until the end of the war and be made in far greater numbers than all previous marks combined, while retaining the F/8 chassis, evidenced a major change in the superstructure, which was completely new. While many detail changes would be introduced on to both the Ausf G and the StuH 42 over the course of that period to accommodate the demands of combat or the need to streamline production, there were no further changes to the armour provision, the main armament or the chassis of the vehicle.

The superstructure was extended outwards over the track guards, this widening occurring behind the gun mantlet. It was also slightly higher than that of the previous variants, being necessary to permit the fitting of a modified ventilator in the roof. However, the greatest change was to the roof, which was completely new. This was removable to permit servicing of the main armament and was secured to the walls of the superstructure by countersunk set screws to rectangular strips welded on the nearside of the roof, slightly to the rear of the transverse centreline.

For the first time the StuG commander was provided with a cupola, with seven visor blocks. He was also provided with a mount for a scissors periscope. The hinge for the hatch

BELOW An image that recurs quite frequently. Officers and men take the opportunity for a jaunt on the new StuG III Ausf G.

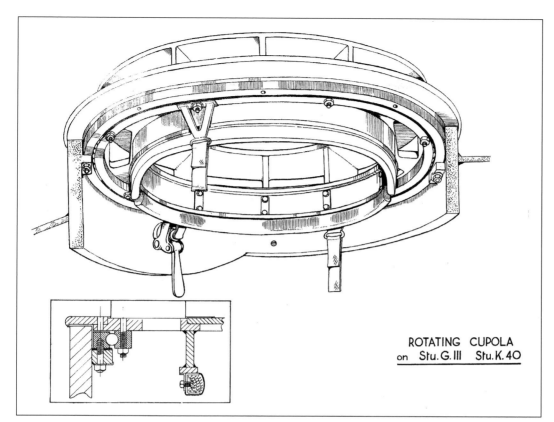

ROTATING CUPOLA
on Stu.G.III Stu.K.40

on the cupola was located above the fourth periscope. This was the case even when the StuG III G was equipped with a fully rotating cupola. This was not a constant fitting, with Alkett adding it to the StuGs built by them between December 1942 and November 1943, and MIAG between February 1943 and November of that same year. The introduction of a fixed cupola from September 1943 had been dictated by the shortage of ball bearings. With this problem alleviated, the fully rotatable cupola was reintroduced in August 1944 and was to remain a standard feature until the end of production. It is of note that a British Army report of November 1944 commented on the StuG they had under evaluation, that it was the first time they had seen the rotatable cupola on the StuG Ausf G and assumed it to be a new feature. It is reasonable to infer that the StuG Ausf Gs they had seen prior to that date had fixed cupolas, having been built in the 11-month period when ball bearings were in short supply. This is likely to have been the case as until the beginning of the Normandy Campaign in June 1944, all StuG Ausf Gs encountered by them would have been in the

Sicilian/Italian Campaigns, which began in July 1943.

Despite the reintroduction of the rotating cupola in September 1944, the resulting problematic supply situation by this stage of the conflict meant that it was not always possible to fit all StuGs with this feature, whereupon the fixed cupola was then fitted. However, combat experience showed that it was vulnerable to enemy fire as it could be penetrated, torn off and on occasions would fall into the fighting compartment. To provide protection, Alkett introduced a cast armour plate deflector, which was welded in place just ahead the cupola in September 1943 with MIAG following suit three months later. As an expedient, crews in the field operating StuGs built before they were so fitted created their own cupola protection by employing concrete.

The walls of the superstructure of the first series of the Ausf G, which employed the 200 chassis originally built for the F/8, had sloping walls of a greater angle than on those that followed and were constructed between December 1942 and February 1943. The greatest change was, however, to the roof,

which was completely new. This was made removable to permit servicing of the main armament and was secured to the walls of the superstructure by countersunk set screws to rectangular strips welded on the nearside of the roof, slightly to the rear of the transverse centreline.

To the right of the cupola and in front of the loader's hatch was a machine-gun shield that was now fitted as standard. This was normally carried lying flat on the roof in front of the loader's hatch when not in use. This fitting obtained through to mid-1944 when a new roof layout was introduced, incorporating provision for a rotating machine gun operable from within the hull when the StuG was closed down. Provision was also made for a circular hatch to accommodate the planned close-in defence weapon that did not become available, albeit in small numbers, before the end of 1944.

Armour thicknesses and angles

The drawings of the distribution and angles of the armour plate combined with the same as set out on the table give a comprehensive picture of the structure of a captured example of a MIAG-built StuG III Ausf G, as evaluated by the British Army School of Tank Technology in 1944 and carried the Fahrgestall Nummer 96158.

ABOVE An interesting picture to show what tank crewmen in all armies did (and do) – adopt weaponry to fire as they best see fit according to circumstance. This StuG loader has attached the onboard MG34 to the top of the MG shield, probably to permit better visibility when firing. The casual pose of both crewmen suggests that they do not see themselves as being in danger from enemy fire. Another StuG stands alongside them – note the extra aerials and the front part of the muzzle brake.

BELOW Armour plate. Cross-section of the StuG III Ausf G to illustrate the thickness of hull armour and fighting compartment.

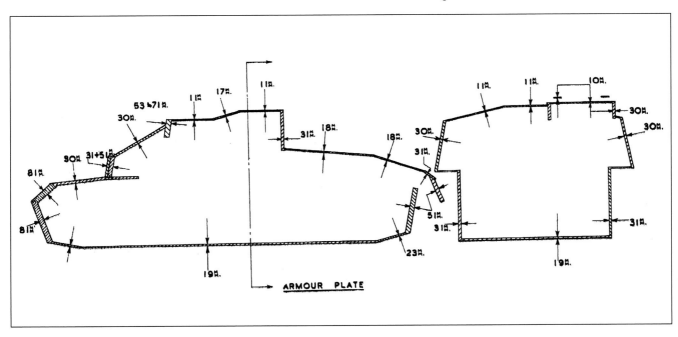

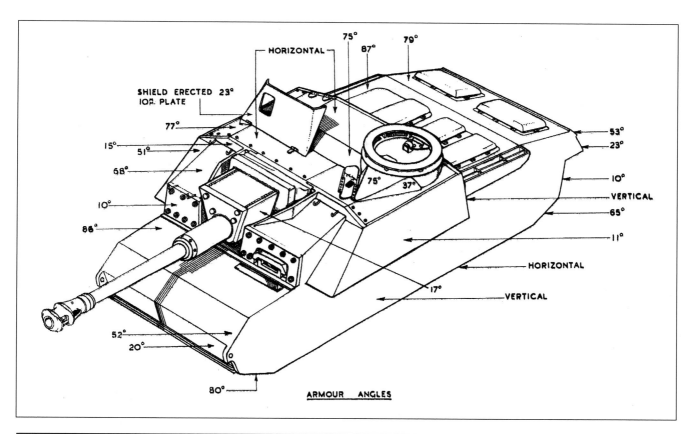

ARMOUR ANGLES

ABOVE Armour plate angles on the StuG III Ausf G.

Position	Basic (mm)	Extra	Angle
Cupola top	10		Horizontal
Cupola front and sides	30		Vertical
F/C top front	11		Horizontal
F/C centre	17		75°
F/C top rear	11		Horizontal
F/C top sides	11		77°
F/C sides	30		11°
F/C rear	31		vertical
F/C front	(sides) 53		15°
F/C	(centre section) 71		15°
Gun mantlet	51		Moveable
Front vertical plate	51	31	10°
Front glacis plate	30		86°
Front nose plate	81		52°
Front lower nose plate	81		20°
Side hull plate	31		Vertical
Top rear plate	18		87°
Top rear engine cover plate	18		79°
Rear engine cover plate (lower)	31		53°
Belly plate (front)	20mm (estimated)		80°
Belly plate (middle)	19		Horizontal
Belly plate (rear)	23		65°
Tail plate (upper)	51		23°
Tail plate (lower)	50		10°

F/C = Fighting Compartment

This table does not include the 5mm *Schürzen* side skirts fitted on all new-build StuG IIIs and StuH 42s from May/June 1943. Older surviving machines were to be retro-fitted by order as of June 1943.

Tracks

ABOVE This StuK40, believed to have belonged to StuGAbt 226, was recovered from a bog in Russia, in 2002. It had fallen through the ice during the retreat in 1944. Note the *Winterketten/ Ostketten.*

(Shutterstock)

The width of the tracks of all StuGs built from March 1941 was 40cm. However, while that was the standard width of the track there were at least four types of track link employed by the StuG III through to the end of production in 1945.

1) The first of these was introduced in March 1941 with the Ausf C and remained in production through to 1945. It was probably the most common type of track employed on the StuG III. Features of the track link included two grooves and a double side-bar. This permitted these tracks to be fitted when conditions required, with hammer-type cleats for grip or it could be fitted with a snow chevron. It had a perforated guide horn.
2) Produced from April 1943 was a new track with four small cut-outs and was equipped with a hollow but non-perforated guide horn.
3) Introduced in December 1943 was a further type of track. This had six chevrons, a double side-bar and a hollow but non-perforated guide horn.

4) The very last type of track introduced on the StuG III appeared in July 1944. Its distinctive features included four less prominent chevrons, double side-bar, four small cut-outs and a hollow but non-perforated track guide.

The extreme weather conditions in Russia in the autumn and winter of 1941/42 had seen the narrow tracks of the StuG III and its corresponding high ground pressure cause real problems in the mud of '*Rasputitsa*' (the 'season of mud') and the winter with its excessive snowfall. In consequence, two specialised tracks were introduced, the purpose of which were to reduce the 'footprint' – that is the ground pressure of the StuG on both mud and snow – permitting them to move more efficiently and not get bogged down.

The first of these, dubbed '*Winterketten*', were first introduced in the winter of 1942/43 and were to be made available and fitted not just to the StuG units, but also to be employed on the Panzer III and Panzer IV. These were

ABOVE *Ostketten* on an unidentified Ausf G.

issued to the StuG and panzer units for winter operations only.

A second 'special' track was issued from May 1944 to units serving on the Eastern Front only. Named '*Ostketten*', these were permanent tracks and were manufactured to be wider from the outset and were thus stronger than '*Winterketten*', where the additions to the outer track link had a tendency to fall off. The '*Ostketten*' were seen on many StuGs throughout the summer of 1944 serving in the East. If StuG units serving in the East after the summer of 1944 found themselves despatched westward, they would be required to surrender their '*Ostketten*'.

Armament – Ausf F/8 and Ausf G

It was the fitting of the longer 75mm StuK L/43 in the Ausf F and F/8, and the 75mm StuK L/48 in the Ausf G, that saw the designation of the StuG changed from SdKfz 142, as employed on the short-barrelled machines, to that of the SdKfz 142/1.

Production of the StuK 40 L/43 main gun for the Ausf F ran from March to May 1942 for the Ausf F, and the StuK 40 L/48 from June 1942 through to the end of the conflict. The gun was developed by Rheinmetall-Borsig.

As was noted earlier, as there was no substantial difference in the placement of the L/42 or the L/48 weapon within the hull of the StuG or of the ammunition used by the three variants, they will be treated together. As can be seen from the drawing showing the placement of the StuK 40 within the fighting compartment, it occupied the greater part of that space.

The notion of adapting the StuG to accommodate the longer 75mm L/70 main gun that was mounted on the Panther tank and on the designated successor to the StuG III, in the form of the Jagdpanzer IV/70, was explored. Apart from the problem of accommodating the larger weapon within the fighting compartment, it was also ascertained that the greater weight of 500kg would impose stress on the engine. This would in turn feed through to reducing the manoeuvrability of the machine. In addition,

This profile of the interior of the StuG III Ausf G shows how much of the fighting compartment was taken up by the 75mm StuK 40 L/48 main gun. It is easy enough to see how it was that the interior of the StuG was simply too small to take the longer 75mm L/70 as was mounted on the Panther.

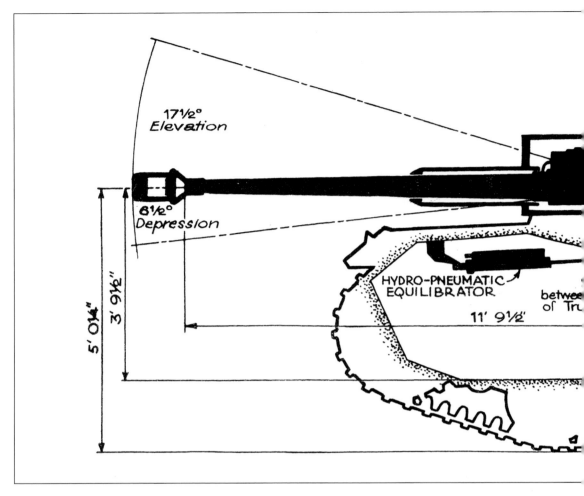

BELOW Ausf G with 75mm StuK 40 L/48, Finnish Army.

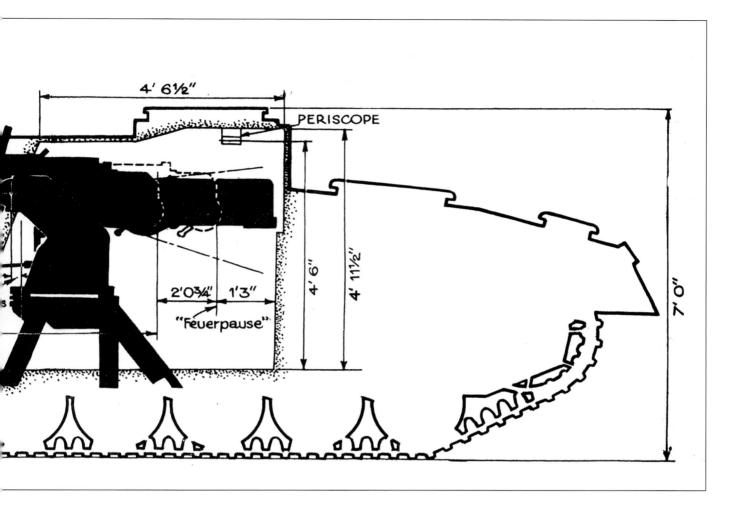

due to the amount of dust thrown up by the firing of the L/70 weapon, the rate of fire would necessarily be reduced. There was also a loss of gun adjustment and the need to provide for a more complex barrel mounting.

The 75mm StuK 40 gun was installed within the fighting compartment of the StuG on a pedestal mounting well forward relative to the trunions. The forward ends of the recoil cylinders for the weapon were carried within an external, armoured mantlet.

However, there were detail differences between the StuK 40 L/43 and the StuK 40 L/48 and these are noted below:

a) On the StuK 40 L/43, a number were not equipped with a hydraulic safety switch, whereas all were so equipped on the L/48.

b) Differences in the gunner's seat: on the L/43 it was not adjustable and had a fixed back support, whereas for the L/48 the seat was both adjustable and had a folding back support.

c) On the L/43, the barrel rifling increased from 6 to 9° over its length while on the L/48 it was the same as for the L/43 on the first 400 guns. Thereafter it was set at a standard 7° over the length.

d) The L/43 had no gun carriage lock on the roller grip. In the case of the L/48 weapon a number were not equipped with such a feature, although beyond a certain point the newer guns were equipped with travel locks on both sides.

e) All L/43 guns were equipped with a traverse lock on the traverse gear, but this was so only on some of the early L/48 weapons. Later guns had a travel lock with a bayonet lock.8. gear.

f) The gunsight was mounted lower to the left on all L/43 weapons, whereas on all L/48 guns the sight was located higher and to the right.

In our description of the gun we will move from the muzzle brake backwards along the barrel and on to the main body of the weapon within the hull.

It was a maxim impressed on all StuG crews that the main gun could not be fired without there being a muzzle brake fitted. The purpose of this was to reduce the recoil of the gun within the hull when fired. This was realised by each chamber, of which there were two, having a baffle plate on its forward part, the purpose of which was to vent the gases released by the firing of the gun out of the sides of each chamber, the consequence of which was to reduce the recoil of the gun.

The shape of these muzzle brakes varied over the lifetime of the production of the Ausf F, F/8 and Ausf G and were, apart from a very few F/8s equipped with the same ball-shaped, single-chambered muzzle brake as found on the PzKpfw IV Ausf F/2 in September 1942, of a two-chamber type of different shapes and with blast faces and chambers of differing sizes. They were sourced from a variety of suppliers who produced their muzzle brakes to differing designs and modified them to take account of feedback from the operators. All, however, were sized and threaded to that of the barrel of the gun.

The gun barrel was of one piece and could be separated from the breech, which was easily removed. The primary structures of the main gun – that is, the barrel cradle, the recoil cylinder and the recuperator, were protected by an armoured mantlet. This was bolted to the barrel cradle. Both Alkett and MIAG used a box-type mantlet, although the former replaced theirs with a cast armoured steel *Saukopf* mantlet from December 1943 through to September 1944. Although the shape for the mantlet fitted by Alkett after that date stayed the same, a distinguishing feature was that it was fitted with an aperture for a coaxial MG34. This, however, was not always fitted. The mantlets on MIAG-built machines retained the box-type through to the end of production in 1945. Not always observable by virtue of its position was a tarpaulin that protected the space between the mantlet and the front of the fighting compartment to prevent the ingress of rainwater. This was fitted by both companies from December 1943 onwards.

BELOW A scene repeated very often on a daily basis. An SdKfz 253 has brought forward ammunition to the front line to resupply the StuG in the picture. The 253 would also normally tow a Sonderanghanger ammunition trailer to supplement that carried by the 253.

The gun was located on a cradle that was attached to the floor of the fighting compartment. A counterbalance was fitted so as to equalise the weight to the fore of the gun trunnions.

The breech itself was of a semi-automatic falling block breech so that it opened automatically in the course of its recoil run-out. It then ejected the empty shell casing, which dropped into the spent shell sack. In combat, the floor of the StuG could be littered with spent cases, the sack only holding a few, so the loader would need to eject them out of his open hatch to permit movement within the fighting compartment. The gun itself was fired electrically, with the trigger to facilitate this being located on the hand traverse wheel. To elevate the gun, the aimer employed a geared crescent-shaped device, which permitted a range from minus 6° through to plus 17°. The traverse mechanism was also a geared device and allowed the main gun to be traversed 10° either side of the gun centreline.

The 75mm StuK 40 L/43 and L/48 both had sights that were slaved to the movement of the gun. The first of these, and the one most commonly used, was the Selbstfahrlafetten-Zielfornrohr 1a gunsight. It was this sight that was employed by the gunner for direct firing at visible targets such as an enemy tank or fixed target. The other sight was the Rundblickfernrohr 32 or 36 periscope. This was used for indirect targeting, for example when the StuG was firing from a covered position. Naturally, it was the former that was employed far more frequently.

Ammunition

The ammunition employed with the 75mm L/43 was the same as that used on the StuG Ausf G.

1) **75mm SprGr Patr 34 –** The standard high-explosive round carried by the StuG F, F/8 and G. It was fitted with an AZ 23 impact fuse.
2) **75mm PzGr Patr 39 –** The standard Armour Piercing Ballistic Cap (APCBC) used by both the StuG and the PzKpfw IV using the L/43, and L/48 main gun.
3) **75mm PzGr Patr 40 –** A 'special' round by

virtue of it only being employed infrequently due to it having a tungsten core. Although the round was highly effective in penetrating enemy armour, tungsten was a metal in short supply, hence its designation as a *Sondermunition* to be used mainly against heavy tanks. Thomas Anderson notes that this factor impacted on its employment such that in the second half of 1942, StuGs and Panzer IVs only employed 6,420 rounds in combat.
4) **75mm PzGr Patr 40 (W) –** This was a round employed against the same targets as the Patr 40 and was externally identical to it. However, its core was of hardened steel rather than tungsten and was used only when the Patr 40 shell was in short supply. Its penetrative performance was inferior to that of the tungsten-cored ammunition.
5) **75mm Gr Patr 38 HL/B, 75mm Gr Patr 38 HL/C –** This was a Hohlladungsgeschosse – that is, a HEAT (High Explosive Anti-Tank) shaped charge round. Although it could be effective, its usefulness was reduced by its low muzzle velocity and high trajectory.
6) **75mm NbGr Patr –** This was a smoke shell.

Whereas the StuG Ausf F and F/8 both officially carried 44 rounds of 75mm ammunition, the Ausf G was able by virtue of its bigger fighting compartment to carry 54 rounds. However, crews frequently adapted the ammunition storage provision so as to carry a larger complement of rounds when going into combat. The diagram showing the ammunition storage within the Ausf G (see page 70) was produced by the British Army and illustrates the standard carriage of a full load of 75mm ammunition within the fighting compartment. The need to carry more rounds was officially recognised by both Alkett and MIAG and attempts were made to find the space within the fighting compartment to increase even further the number that could be carried. By March 1944, drawings showing how to increase storage to between 73 and 76 rounds were with the producers. The intention was to modify existing racks to take the larger number of rounds, although this was abandoned because it was deemed unnecessary as it was enough to recognise that 'the crews have their own tricks and succeed in loading far more rounds'. It was even noted that by leaving it to the units in the field to extemporise as they best saw fit, 'one brigade was able to stow 120 rounds using this approach'.

Communications equipment

All StuGs were provided with an internal intercom and this can be seen in a number of the images in this text.

The radio equipment fitted to the StuG III Ausf F, F/8 and G was identical. In all cases they were fitted either with a FuG 15 or FuG 16 radio.

The former was an ultra short wave (USW) receiver and operated in the frequency bands between 23,000 and 24,950 kilocycles (kc). The latter was a 10W transmitter and operated in the frequency bands 23,000–24,950kc. In addition a USW receiver also operated in the same frequency bands. Both of these radios employed a 2m road aerial.

If a StuG was being employed as a command vehicle at either the battalion or brigade staff level, it carried a FuG 8 30W radio transmitter and receiver. As in the case of command panzers in the latter part of the war, a command StuG could be recognised by it being equipped with a Star Antenna D. This was carried in the aerial position behind the loader's hatch. The FuG 8 permitted the StuG battalion commander to communicate using voice up to 60km and to employ Morse code up to 100km.

Sturmhaubitze III Ausf G SdKfz 142/2

As was noted in the section on the Sturmhaubitze in Chapter 2, production of this variant of the StuG Ausf G did not begin until March 1943.

Exernally there was no difference in the appearance of the two machines apart from the obvious one of the gun on the Sturmhaubitze being shorter than that of the standard StuG. This obtained through to the beginning of 1944 when the large *Saukopf* mantlet was introduced. The only other significant change before production ended in 1945 was the deletion of the muzzle brake on the 105mm gun in September 1944. However, on older Sturmhaubitze, a damaged muzzle brake could be replaced with one taken from either the FH18 or the le FH18/40 field howitzers. The Sturmhaubitze was also equipped (when available) from late 1944 with the remote-controlled machine gun mounted in front of the loader's hatch.

Internally, the changes were to accommodate a smaller number of 105mm rounds of which 36 rounds – some 8 less than officially carried by the StuG Ausf G with the 75mm main gun – were carried. As with crews of the standard StuG, those of the Sturmhaubitze were also prone to carry more than that officially prescribed.

RIGHT A Sturmhaubitze 42 crew load shells in Russia, autumn 1943. *(Bundesarchiv)*

Main gun specification

Calibre (actual)	10.49cm
Length of piece (excl muzzle brake)	115.75in (28 cals)
Length of barrel (incl muzzle brake)	130.91in
No of grooves	32
Twist	RH increasing 6° to 12°
Length of bore (from breech to muzzle)	106.5in
Weight of barrel (complete)	0.7 tons
Weight of gun and cradle	1.7 tons
Elevation	-6° to +20°
Traverse	20°
Buffer fluid content	6.5 litres (11.5 pints)
Normal recoil	600mm (23.6in)
Metal to metal	640mm (25.2in)
Recuperator fluid content	4.6 litres (7.1 pints)
Air pressure	45 + or - 3 atmos
Compensator fluid content	2.4 litres (4.2 pints)
Air pressure	50 atmos (760lb/sq in)
Breech block	horizontal sliding wedge
Muzzle velocity (firing long-range shell with Supercharge)	1,770ft/sec
Maximum range	13,480yd

Ammunition

1) High-explosive shell

The Sturmhaubitze 42 could fire four types of HE shell. The long-range shell is covered separately.

The four types of HE shell are as follows:

1) FH Gr;
2) FH Gr 38;
3) FF Gr 38 Stg;
4) FH Gr FES (iron driving band).

All of these were fused with percussion fuses AZ 23 (0.15) and AZ 23 (0.25) or T and P fuses Dopp ZS/60s and Dopp S60 Fl.

2) Hollow-charge shell

Three types of hollow-charge shell could be fired:

a) 100mm Gr 39 rot HL/A. Fitted with an AZ38 fuse, weight 27lb 3oz.

b) 100mm Gr 39 rot HL/B. Fitted with an AZ38 fuse, weight 26lb 12oz.
c) 100mm Gr 39 rot H1 (deemed obsolete by 1944).

3) Smoke shell

Two types of smoke shell were carried.
1) FH Gr Nb Fitted with a Kl AZ 23 Nb fuse, weight 30lb 14oz.
2) FH Gr 38 Nb Fitted with a Kl AZ 23 Nb fuse, weight 36lb 7oz.
Shell 2) produced a larger smoke cloud than 1).

4) HE/Incendiary shell

1) FH Gr Spr Br equipped with an AZ 23 fuse (0.15) or Dopp Z S/60 Fl, weight 32lb 11oz. This shell was fired with a special charge, the *Fernladung,* and its performance gave the IFH 18 (M) a maximum range of 13,480yd against 11,650yd with the original IFH 18.

Chapter Six

StuG III walk-around

The StuG III Ausf G featured in this chapter was supplied to Finland by the Germans in the summer of 1944. Although an ally of the Third Reich, this did not stop Germany from charging the Finns a higher price for the StuG than those supplied to the Wehrmacht. This particular assault gun was built by Alkett and wears the company's distinctive waffle-type Zimmerit anti-magnetic mine paste.

OPPOSITE Three of this variant of the all-steel return rollers were fitted on either side of the StuG hull. This particular variant was fitted from January 1944 until the end of the war. The holes in the front roller were to both lighten the structure and to permit mud to escape from between the front and rear roller.

The Sturmgeschütz III Ausf G seen in this walk-around is one of the 59 sold to the Finnish Government between June 1943 and July 1944, although 60 had been ordered. The 15 due to be sent from Germany in August 1944 did not materialise as the Finnish and Soviet Governments concluded hostilities in that month. Although it was in Germany's strategic interest to keep Finland in the war against the Soviet Union, it did not stop them levying a surcharge of 50% above that paid by the Wehrmacht for the price of each assault gun.

This StuG was shipped from Danzig to Finland on 6 July 1944. It was finished in the then standard Wehrmacht Sandgelb paint. On arrival it was issued to the 3rd Company of the Finnish Army's Assault Gun Battalion, which was a tank unit and not an artillery unit. The very last Sturmgeschütz did not leave service with the Finns until the end of 1966. They were thus the longest serving of all StuGs, save for the captured examples supplied by Russia to the Syrian Army and encountered by the Israeli Army in the Six-Day War in 1967.

1 Side view of the late model Sturmgeschütz Ausf G, as sold by Germany to Finland in the summer of 1944. Built by Alkett, it was supplied without *Schürzen*.

2 A very clear view of those features that characterised the Ausf G. This was the final model of the assault gun, entering production with Alkett in December 1942, and MIAG the following February. It was the most widely produced variant with 8,416 manufactured by the time production closed down in both factories in April 1945. Alkett also produced a further 1,299 of the Sturmhaubitze III, which differed in armament – carrying a 105mm howitzer instead of the 75mm StuK L/48.

3 Conspicuous on the upper front plate of the StuG is the Notek blackout light. This could be found on most Ausf F and Ausf G assault guns through to the end of the war.

Ps 531-44

4 An expedient used by the Finnish Army as well as the Wehrmacht (see other images in the text) was tree logs employed on the sides of the machines as a form of armour. In the absence of *Schürzen*, the flanks of the fighting compartment were vulnerable to penetration to Soviet anti-tank rifle fire and anti-tank gunfire. While its effectiveness was questionable, the thickness of the wood might be enough to absorb sufficient kinetic energy of an incoming round to give the StuG a chance of survival.

5 A clear rear view of the StuG shows the extent of the *Zimmerit* coating (of which more later). See how the left mudguard is the distance indicator to aid a driver of a vehicle in the StuG's rear. Early variants of the assault gun had spare roadwheels attached to the superstructure, but by the time of the Ausf G these had migrated to the rear deck of the vehicle where two single roadwheels would be carried on two vertical mountings on the two rear engine covers. The railing around the rear deck to aid the crew with stowage was a standard fitting by Alkett from November 1943 and MIAG from May 1944 to the end of the war.

6 This form of idler wheel was introduced by Alkett on the StuGs built by them from March 1941, and on those built by MIAG from the first StuG Ausf G they manufactured in February 1943. It was constructed with a welded steel rim with eight spokes and a cylindrical hub.

7 The track tensioner fitted on the rear of the hull behind the idler wheel. This was standard on all StuG models from the Ausf B through to the Ausf G.

8 One of the six suspension arms that carried the roadwheels on either side of the Panzer III/StuG hull. These were linked and connected to the torsion bars on the inside of the hull.

9 There were two shock absorbers attached to the swing arms of first and sixth roadwheels on either side of the hull. These were the standard shock absorbers fitted on Ausf B to G by both Alkett and MIAG (from February 1943).

10 This type of drive sprocket was fitted from the second production batch of the Ausf A in 1940 through to June 1944 by Alkett, and by MIAG between February and November 1943.

11 StuGs built between June 1940 and May/June 1944 were equipped with these types of roadwheels. Rubber tyres, many of which were made of synthetic rubber, came from a variety of manufacturers, in this case Continental.

12 The very distinctive cast armoured *Saukopf* mantlet was introduced only by Alkett from October 1943 to September 1944. That on the StuH ceased being fitted in August 1944. Thereafter, the StuG III still employed a cast mantlet but it was now equipped with an opening for a machine gun.

13 This slab of armour plate was welded over the driver's visor to give extra protection and also served to screen out snow in the winter. '*Maija*' is in all probability the name of the driver's girlfriend.

14 Concrete added to the front of the fighting compartment armour became a common feature seen on many StuGs on the Eastern Front, especially from 1944 onward. This was added by the crew as a field expedient in the same fashion that other crews welded spare tracks to their machines. Officialdom frowned upon both procedures deeming them to be ineffective. Even if this was the case they must have given the crews a psychological boost, be they German or Finnish.

15 Close-up of the Notek light also permits a good view of the *Zimmerit* applied to this StuG. Although officially sanctioned for adding to the exteriors of selected tanks and assault guns beginning in September 1943, Alkett did not begin applying it to StuGs built in their factory until the last two months of 1943. The distinctive 'waffle' form of the *Zimmerit* allows it to be identified as an Alkett-produced machine. Discontinued in September 1944.

16 This particular form of towing hold was made by extending the hull of the StuG forward and was employed on all machines built on the Ausf F chassis – this included the Ausf G. Alkett used this form from September 1942 through to January 1945, and MIAG from February 1943 through to November 1944.

17 Another view of the towing hold also permits a good view of the track retaining bar that was placed across the front of the hull. Many StuGs carried captured tank tracks – especially from the T-34 – using this feature as added protection. The track is the 40cm, two-grooved, double side-bar that was employed on the StuG III from March 1941 through to April 1945.

18 Another view of the added visor of the Finnish StuG. It also served to provide a sun visor as in Finnish climes the sun could reach a very low angle, dazzling the driver.

19 This type of muzzle brake was fitted to all 75mm StuK 40 L/48 gun barrels between June 1942 with the introduction of the Ausf F and the end of the conflict. The designation Ps 531-44 is a Finnish Army unit marking. Note the cable retainer fitted with the standard butterfly screw on the right-hand track guard.

20 The commander's cupola was only introduced on the StuG III with the Ausf G in December 1942. It was the vulnerability of the cupola to being hit by Soviet fire that led to the creation of a cast shot deflector. For those early Ausf Gs lacking this, information was provided on how to make one from cast concrete.

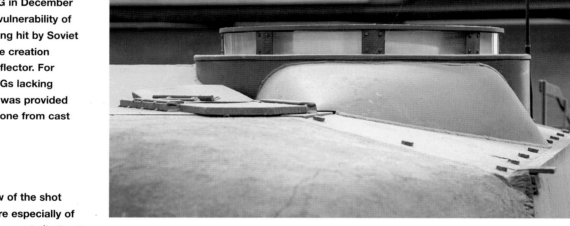

21 A better view of the shot defector and more especially of the commander's cupola. In front of the shot deflector is the safety slide covering the gunner's periscope.

22 This photograph shows how the concrete was trowelled on to the front of the StuG. It was a field modification and it is entirely possible that the Finns copied this by observing German StuGs serving in Finland that probably carried such extra 'armour'. It is unlikely to have been delivered in this fashion as the machines were bought new.

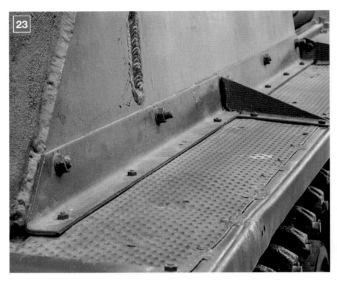

23 The strip along the base of the fighting compartment secured it to the track fender. The screws were undone when, in order to service the main gun, the fighting compartment needed to be lifted up by a crane vehicle.

24 The lifting hook welded to the forward edge of the left-hand air intake just to the rear of the fighting compartment.

25 A clear view of the rear engine deck from the left. In the centre of the vertical plate at the rear of the fighting compartment is the cover for the ventilator fan – this is placed directly behind the gun breech to extract fumes after firing. There are two aerial brackets welded on to the rear wall of the fighting compartment. Normally only one would be carried. The aerial itself was tapered, being 2m in length. Funklenk StuGs carried two aerials as standard. This particular StuG is lacking the spare track retainer that was carried by all StuG III Ausf Gs between December 1943 and the end of production. Given that the Finns retained their surviving StuGs in service for some time after the war, it could well be they simply removed it from this example.

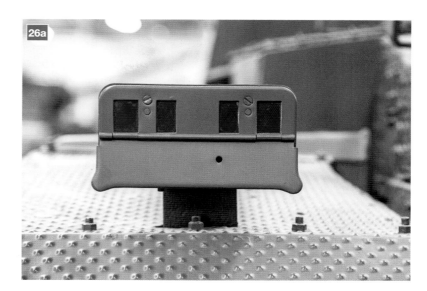

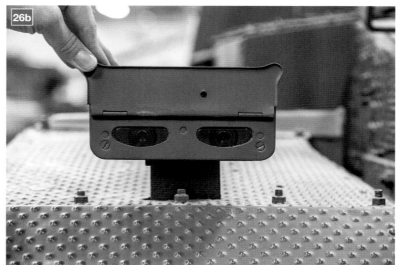

26a and 26b These two images allow a clearer and more detailed perspective of the tail light carried on the StuG's rear left mudflap. In the first, the cover is closed and seen as it would be if the light was on at night. In the second, the cover is lifted to expose the light beneath.

27 A view from the right rear across the back of the engine deck of the StuG. In the foreground it can be seen how the spare wheel is retained on its carrying spike. The engine covers and the deck itself are liberally covered with Alkett's waffle-pattern *Zimmerit*.

28 The engine deck is equipped with three lifting hooks – that seen here between the two rearmost engine covers and the two that were welded on the front of the left- and right-hand side air intakes.

29 The armoured cover of the engine crank position on the rear of the StuG engine deck.

30 This view gives more detailed coverage of the rear of the StuG. The Finnish vehicle code, Ps 531-44 is repeated while below can be seen the two exhaust pipes that are protected with armoured covers.

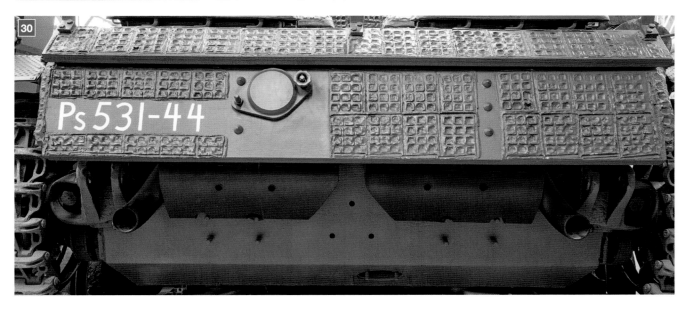

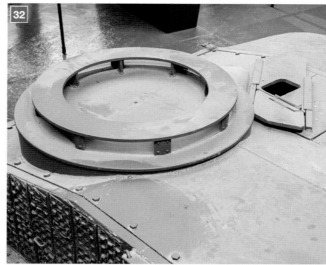

31 This image is dominated by the machine-gun shield in front of the loader's hatch and it is very likely to have been fixed in an upright position by the Finns. Directly in front of the hatch and behind the shield is the circular cover blocking off the fitting for the rotating machine gun. This feature places the manufacturing date of this StuG between May and October 1944.

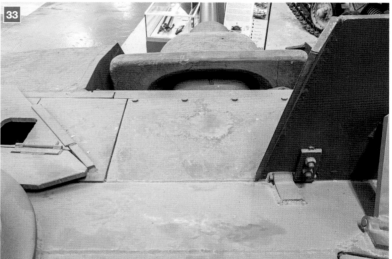

32 This view across the roof of the fighting compartment takes in the cupola but allows us to see in greater detail the hatch through which the gunner raised the telescopic sight that this particular vehicle was fitted with. The cover is open but could be closed to prevent the ingress of water.

33 Missing on this example of the later StuG III Ausf G is the weather protection tarpaulin that was fitted between the mantlet and the top of the fighting compartment.

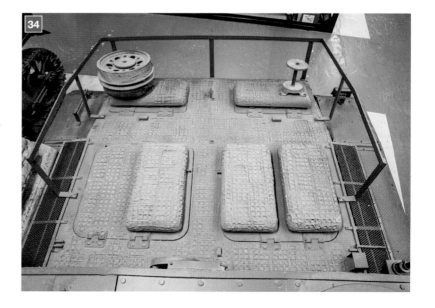

34 The rear deck seen from the top of the fighting compartment allows a detailed view of the armoured engine covers, the spare wheel retainers and deck railing. The large hatches allowed easy access for the mechanics to the Maybach engine.

Chapter Seven

StuG III in combat 1940–43

It was in the first three years of war that the StuG III assault gun acquired its reputation as an infantry support weapon and tank destroyer. However, it was with the longer 75mm gun that the StuG was able to engage and defeat any Soviet armour at range, becoming a highly regarded tank destroyer and claiming a very high number of kills.

OPPOSITE A StuG III G photographed in southern Russia in 1943. It has not been fitted with the rails to mount *Schürzen*. The terrain illustrates how the StuG was able to exploit the range of its gun on the Russian Steppe, the rolling landscape providing little cover for Russian tanks to hide. This was the ideal combat environment for the assault gun through to 1944. *(Alamy)*

105

May 1940–May 1941

The combat career of the Sturmgeschütz III began on 10 May 1940 with the opening of the German assault on France and the Low Countries. As we have seen the actual number that participated was less than the five Sturmbatterien that had been intended. With the attachment of the very first Sturmbatterie 640 to the Grossdeutschland (hereafter GD) Regiment, although intended as but temporary, it was to become permanent, with GD becoming the only Army formation with its own organic StuG Batterie.

Excluding Batterie 640 which, because of its attachment to GD, was no longer counted on the Army's Order of Battle for the StuG Batterien dated 15 April 1940, only three other batteries were actually ready for commitment t o the campaign as of that date. Due to the delays in receipt of equipment – both of StuGs and their support equipment – the Order of Battle noted that Sturmbatterie 659 should have received theirs and be ready as of 20 April. Sturmbatterie 660 was due to be ready for operations on 8 May – just two days before the start of 'Case Yellow'. However, due to the distinct lack of proper support vehicles, particularly of the SdKfz 252 ammunition

resupply half-tracks, this unit received in their stead a number of Panzer I substitutes converted to ammunition carriers, being designated Munitionstransportkompanie 601. These Panzer Is were well-worn vehicles and their serviceability throughout the campaign was poor. Finally, the last unit, Sturmbatterie 665, was established the day before 'Case Yellow' began. In consequence it entered combat just over a month later, on 10 June 1940.

Given that no more than 24 Sturmgeschütz saw service in the French Campaign and that very few after-action reports on their performance exist, reconstructing a coherent account of their role is difficult. The first assault guns to see action belonged to what was now Grossdeutschland's own Sturmbatterie – the former Sturmbatterie 640. The regiment had arrived at the river Meuse at Sedan alongside the 1st Panzer Division and on 13 May, along with GD and the Sturmpionier Abteilung 43, it was tasked with crossing the river and breaking through the enemy bunkers on the far side of the Meuse. Even though the Luftwaffe had directed extensive raids at the defences on the far side, the French manning many of the bunkers were initially able to prevent the German assault boats from crossing. It was

RIGHT At the very start of 'Case Yellow' the 3-ton APCs attached to Sturmbatterie 640, now attached to the Grossdeutschland Regiment (GD), cross the border into Luxembourg on 10 May 1940.

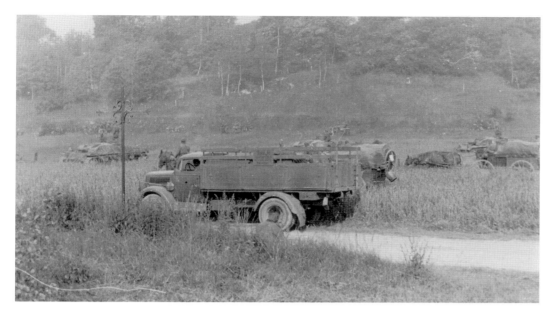

here and now that the StuG saw its very first service. They were brought forward and ordered to blast Bunker 211 from across the river but to no avail. The river was eventually crossed and the bunker line stormed. The StuG Batterie was involved in the tank battle at Stonne on the afternoon of 14 May where the Germans found that the 75mm L/24 main gun of the StuG and Panzer IV could not penetrate the armour of the French heavy Char IB-BIS tank. This was

eventually resolved with the Germans defeating the French force, but it was a salutary lesson for the Germans as to the limitations of their weaponry – a matter that would be repeated again in Russia the following year.

Thereafter the StuGs of GD were involved in the thrust to the coast and were in action at Amiens and Dunkirk. In the second phase of operations the Sturmbatterie was involved in the drive into south-eastern France, being

BELOW An SdKfz 251 armoured personnel carrier of GD leads a StuG III Ausf A through a deserted French village on its advance towards the Atlantic coast.

RIGHT A short halt in the rapid advance across northern France – a Zug of Sturmbatterie 640 had drawn up amid rain.

BELOW The destruction of the bridge in the background of this image by the retreating French forces saw the German Army engineers construct a pontoon substitute. To enable the StuG to cross it had to be able to carry a 20-ton assault gun. As we shall see, in Russia not all bridges constructed by the engineers could be crossed as they were not intended to carry that weight.

instrumental in the capture of the city of Lyons. It was here that the news of the French surrender was received and operations ceased.

Sturmbatterie 659 found itself in combat as early as 10 and 11 May in the fighting to capture a crossing of the Meuse. With the crossing secured the Batterie advanced, helping to secure the town of Laon and was after this involved in fighting to secure a crossing over

the heavily defended Oise-Aisne Canal. This was achieved in the early hours of 1 June, when the Batterie captured a French defensive position at Chateau-Porcien, thereby aiding the capture of the crossing over the canal and shortly after the town of Juneville. The StuGs also proved invaluable in helping to secure the city of Chalons, thereafter capturing the French Army Training Ground at Mourmelon. A

LEFT A Zug of Sturmbatterie 659 has drawn up in a field somewhere in France. This unit entered combat on 10 June, having only finished forming a short while before. An SdKfz 253 of the unit is in the foreground of the image.

rapid redeployment followed with the Batterie assisting another infantry division whose advance had stalled at St Dizier. This was resurrected as the StuGs broke through the enemy defences with the town being secured.

In the second phase of the campaign the Batterie assisted in the capture of the Langres Plateau on 15 June and the following day helped secure the town of Besancon. Thereafter, the StuGs pushed forward to Belfort and by the time of the Armistice the Batterie had arrived at the Franco-Swiss border.

Sturmbatterie 660 did not enter combat until a few days after the Campaign in the West began, arriving at Nousonville to the north of Sedan. Tasked with assisting the 3rd Infanterie Division to secure crossings across the Meuse, the six assault guns executed this task by driving along the banks of the river and shooting up the French defences that were preventing the crossings from taking place. Having silenced the enemy on the far bank the StuGs then shot smoke shells to screen the infantry as they crossed the river in their rubber assault craft. In an early testimonial to the effectiveness of the assault guns the battalion commander later stated that: 'I don't believe that we would have managed to make the crossing and then silence the enemy defensive positions without the decisive support of the Sturmgeschütze.'

On 16 May the Sturmbatterie was attached to the 8th Panzer Division and in the days following: '. . . they were ordered to smash

their way through to the English Channel with the tanks. French tanks which challenged the Sturmgeschütze in the fighting were destroyed. The Battery still had not suffered any losses.'

Having reached and pushed through the town of St Quentin the Batterie was then attached to the Waffen SS and involved in the fighting that saw the British counter-attack at Arras beaten back on 21 May. Resumption of the offensive saw the StuGs reach Hazebrouck on 28 May. British forces engaged the Germans in heavy fighting but this was broken by the Sturmbatterie. The 'Halt Order' issued to the Panzer formations at this time permitted the 660th to spend a few days in overhauling their vehicles. It also saw the formation jettisoning their Panzer I munitions carriers, which they had been issued in lieu of the SdKfz 253 half-tracks. These old panzers were worn out, unreliable and not up to the task they had been allotted.

The resumption of operations saw the Batterie attached to the 6th Panzer Division for the second phase of the operation. On 9 June the Batterie helped the forced crossing of the river Aisne and thence the Ardennes Canal on the night of 10/11 June. It was in this engagement that the Batterie suffered its first loss with a StuG knocked out by repeated hits from French 25mm anti-tank guns. Having broken through the French defences along the Aisne, German forces then pushed southward and between 14 and 19 June Sturmbatterie 660 was involved almost continuously in

ABOVE While the standard French 25mm anti-tank gun could create some severe gouges in the frontal armour of a StuG it rarely penetrated it.

BELOW A StuG detachment advances through a damaged French village. Both the top of the fighting compartment and the main gun are covered by tarpaulin to prevent the ingress of water from the rain.

action against French forces. Two StuGs were knocked out by French anti-tank guns but these were not 'write-offs', being subsequently repaired and returned to service.

Having crossed the river Marne at Dizier, the Batterie assisted in the capture of Epinal on 19 June. It was then withdrawn and placed in reserve, where it was when the news was announced of the French surrender

The last of the four Sturmbatterien to be committed to the French Campaign was Sturmbatterie 665. In consequence of its later formation it was still in the process of being trained and equipped at Jüterborg on 10 May. It was finally deemed 'combat ready' in time for the second phase of operations and was committed to action in the Vosges mountains region. In the same fashion that the French High Command had deemed the Ardennes impassable for tanks, they had for the same reason not stationed any in the Vosges region so the six assault guns of 665 did not have to face any French armour. However, there were extensive bunker positions that needed to be breached and in this the German infantry operating with the StuGs found their employment exemplary. The StuGs were involved in this fashion until 17 June when the fighting came to an end.

Post-combat assessment

Given the small number of assault guns employed in the French Campaign and the brevity of the actual combat operations, a detailed and extensive evaluation was not possible. Nonetheless, there was an appreciation of the new machine, which it must be assumed had been arrived at by at least some feedback from the front lines, such that the Chief of Army Equipment in a communiqué to the Ordnance Department stated that: 'The honourable Commander-in-Chief of the Army places special emphasis on the increase of Sturmgeschütz output by all means exceeding the hitherto forecasts. We ask the ordnance department for their delivery of proposals.'

One of the more revealing documents was a German report that had been released by the Propaganda Department concerning the role of the Sturmbatterie 640 when operating with the GD regiment. This was in turn

LEFT A StuG III of Sturmbatterie 659 has drawn up at the side of a French road in the closing stages of the French Campaign in June 1940.

CENTRE With the French surrender the crews took the time to rehabilitate their charges after the short, sharp campaign. Belonging to Sturmbatterie 659, this particular machine is replete with numerous spare tracks and other paraphernalia that crews inevitably accrue during the course of their operations.

BELOW At the end of 1940, Sturmbatterie 665 was despatched to East Prussia along with three other Batterien. Here they engage in training as part of the preparations for Operation 'Barbarossa'.

ABOVE Both Panzer and StuG units often had their own unit marking – in this case the StuG wears a unicorn on its fighting compartment side denoting this assault gun belongs to Sturmbatterie 667.

evaluated by American military intelligence for whom the existence of the StuG was as yet unknown. Running to a number of paragraphs, the second is of great value for our concerns. It says:

'The author [sic] indicates that in the particular engagement [described in the report] this assault artillery fulfilled the mission for which it was designed. Conversations with military personnel and in the context of other articles published in German military periodicals confirms the conclusion that this assault artillery gave important and timely assistance to the leading infantry elements on many occasions on the Western Front in the spring of 1940.'

It was also noted by the US analysts that: '. . . because this weapon is completely armoured, it conforms to the commonly accepted definition of a tank'.

Certainly a misperception that was shared by some formation commanders can be gleaned by how some of the Sturmbatterien were used. They were indeed employed in leading the advance of a particular thrust into enemy territory – normally the prerogative of the armoured forces. It could be said that this was probably inevitable, even though it did not accord with the accepted doctrine as to how the StuG should be employed. This particular matter was returned to in an OKH document of January 1941 which stated: '. . . despite their actual purpose, Sturmgeschütz were often used as tanks well ahead of the infantry. *This commitment is wrong* [author's emphasis]. By doing so, Sturmgeschütz will have the value of solely fighting as stand-in tanks, which for certain will be attacked from the flanks by the enemy anti-tank defences.'

Contained in this short paragraph are issues that would characterise the operations of the Sturmartillerie down to the war's end. The simple fact was that once engaged in large-scale combat operations – as the StuG units would next be in Russia, just six months later – it was inevitable that StuGs would be used as tanks and were, as in the case of the

RIGHT The crew of this StuG A from Sturmbatterie 665 take a breather from operations in France. All wear the beret as also worn at this time by most tankers in the panzer divisions. Although the StuG is employing the original 38cm-wide tracks, it has been fitted already with the wider 40cm roadwheels in anticipation of receiving the same size track.

setting up of Vorausabteilungen (impromptu combat formations) to achieve specific combat objectives. The purity of doctrine was ignored as needs demanded.

Expanding the Sturmartillerie

Between the end of the Campaign in the West and Operation 'Barbarossa' the Sturmartillerie was reorganised. The issue of Table of Organisation KStN 446 on 8 July 1940 saw the creation of the Sturmgeschütz Abteilung (so officially named in January 1941). This mandated the StuGAbt to be equipped with three Batterien of six assault guns in each. There were now 3 x 18-ton Zugkraftwagen recovery half-tracks with the staff battery and the 3 x SdKfz 251s were changed for 3 x 3-ton SdKfz II half-tracks.

Between October 1940 and April 1941 the following Sturmgeschütz Abteilungen were raised:

1940		1941	
StuGAbt No	Month established	StuGAbt No	Month established
184	October	203	January
185	August	210	March
190	October	226	April
191	October	201	April
192	November		
197	November		

The Balkans Campaign

Although in the months following the fall of France a number of Sturmabteilungen went through the motions of practising for an invasion of the British Isles, they were at best tentative and with the postponing of the operation a small number of Sturmartillerie Abteilungen was employed in the Balkans Campaign. Four Abteilungen were committed to the invasion of Greece and Yugoslavia that began on 6 April 1941.

Compared with what was to come in the East just a few months later, this operation was both limited in scope and extent. Of the Abteilungen committed, Nos 184 and 197 were assigned to the attack on Yugoslavia, being attached to Army Group Weichs. Sensing what was to come the Yugoslav Army blew up the bridges over which the StuGs would have had to cross and these were not reconstructed by the engineer troops until 17 April, by which time the Yugoslavs had surrendered.

StuGAbt 190 and 191 advanced into Greece from their deployment position in Bulgaria. They quickly ran into the well-engineered and heavily defended 'Metaxas' Line thereby being unable to advance as rapidly on their objective of the city of Salonika as they had hoped for. Nonetheless, the StuGs were employed in their designed role of infantry support as they were used to destroy, one by one, the bunkers they came across as they advanced through the

LEFT StuG Abteilung 197 was one of the new assault gun formations raised after the French Campaign and constituted in the winter of 1940–41 at Jüterborg. Its combat debut was in the Balkans Campaign. This formation employed a stylised eagle embracing cannon barrels in its claws as the battalion unit marking.

RIGHT A StuG III of StuGAbt 184 crosses a small stream in the course of its advance into Yugoslavia, but it did not see extensive combat.

BELOW Certainly an image for the scale modellers. This StuG of Abteilung 191 has a large store of fuel carried in jerricans on the engine deck and spare road wheels. The use of a tarpaulin was very sensible given how dusty Greek roads were. This Abteilung advanced into Greece via Bulgaria.

Greek positions. The river Nestos was then crossed and the German advance resumed. On the 12th the Abteilung was attached to the 2nd Panzer Division and the following day it reached its objective of Salonika. The StuGAbt was involved in further fighting but with the capture of Athens the campaign ended. The 3rd Batterie of the StuG Abteilung took part in the victory parade in the city on 3 May.

The four participating StuG Abteilungen each returned to be prepared for what was to be their ultimate trial. Far from being a campaign that would be 'over before Christmas' this new war, in the East, would only end when Berlin fell four years later.

The Ost Front

There were few in the German political leadership or in the Wehrmacht who doubted that it would take little more than the nine weeks Hitler had allotted to the campaign to defeat the Soviet Union. When launched on 22 June 1941, Operation 'Barbarossa' was the largest land invasion in history. Three million men and 3,538 tanks and other armoured vehicles were employed with the latter figure including some 272 Sturmgeschütz. These were dispersed, as were the panzers, across the three Army Groups that represented the organisational foci of the German assault on the Russian state.

Of these, the largest was Army Group Centre, which was tasked with the rapid destruction of major Red Army formations in Belorussia so as to prevent their retreat eastwards, beyond the river Dnieper. To facilitate this, the Army Group had been given two Panzergruppen. Unsurprisingly, this formation had also been allocated the largest number of StuG Abteilungen, with these being assigned to the Heerestruppen. That is, most StuG units were assigned to an Army and then allocated on a temporary basis to infantry and panzer units as needs demanded, then taken back again, and then re-allocated. This accounts for the manner with which some StuG units moved very frequently from one unit to another in a short space of time. The total also included those StuGs serving with Grossdeutschland and also the StuG Lehr. There were no reserve StuG formations at all at the time of the invasion.

While this commitment of the totality of the StuG strength suggests that a large number were available, in truth the total number would never be enough to cater for the great demand from the infantry for their services. This was especially so once the first encirclements of Soviet forces had been achieved and the ferocity with which the Red Army fought to break out of them had to be contended with. It became evident, very quickly, that the fighting in the East was unlike anything the German Army had had to deal with until then. With many units unwilling to surrender and fighting to the last man, with bypassed units continuing to offer resistance it lent a savagery to this new war of a sort not experienced in earlier campaigns.

A breakdown of the allocation of StuG formations as of 22 June 1941 was as follows:

Army Group	Army	StuG Abteilung	StuG Batterien
North	16		5
	Pz.Gr.4	–	–
	18	1	–
Total		1	5
Centre	4	2	–
	Pz.Gr.2	2	–
	9	2	–
	Pz.Gr.3	–	–
Total		6	0
South	11	1	–
	17	1	–
	Pz.G.1	2	–
Total		4	0

Nonetheless, these StuG formations became very overstretched as their services were constantly called upon to help the infantry secure the encirclement of large numbers of Soviet divisions at Uman and later Kiev.

To give some insight into the nature of the operations carried out by the StuG Abteilungen in the opening phase of the Russian Campaign, we will focus on a number of those committed to be representative of the whole.

StuGAbt 184 – Army Group Centre, June–October 1941

After its involvement in the Balkan Campaign, StuGAbt 184 had been despatched to the Arys Training Camp via Judenburg, where it was resupplied and underwent training for five days prior to being sent eastward. Having been subordinated to Army Group Centre, it was deployed to the

BELOW A StuG III of StuGAbt 177 leads a line of support vehicles across the bridge into Russia on 22 June 1941. StuGAbt 177 was one of eight StuG Abteilungen operating with the two Panzergruppen allocated to Army Group Centre.

west of Suwalki in the days leading up to the invasion, but on 22 June it found itself operating on the right wing of Army Group North.

Operations over the next few weeks were characterised by long route marches and intense combat, which saw the assault guns of the battalion involved in quite a few tank battles. This was hardly surprising as the German estimate for the total number of tanks possessed by the Red Army was woefully short of the mark. Even though the bulk of the many thousands being employed by the Russians were tanks of the T-26 and BT series, and thus easily dealt with by the short 75mm main gun of the StuG, they had the same problems as did the panzers when it came to dealing with the much more modern T-34 medium and KV heavy tanks that were far fewer in number but a more significant danger.

The first major armoured encounter occurred just a day after the invasion when the Russians launched heavy counter-attacks against the German VIII and XX Army Corps near Grodno. Conducted by the Soviet 11th Mechanised and 6th Mechanised Corps with a large number of T-34 and KVs and some 500 of the lighter T-26s and BT 5s and 7s, the battle raged for

two days. For the first time the Germans found that even the 75mm mounted on the Panzer IV and StuG III had great difficulty defeating the Russian heavies. Nonetheless, by dint of rapid movement and the concentration of fire on those areas of the 'heavies' that the limited experience acquired in the battle had shown the Germans to be the most vulnerable, this Soviet effort was defeated. The StuGs of Abteilung 184 had found themselves employed in this battle in a manner that would become ever more frequent as the Russian Campaign wound on, as de facto tank destroyers. Some measure of the ferocity of this large encounter was the request made by Colonel Erhard Raus in command of a Kampfgruppe of the 6th Panzer Division, for the emergency resupply of the armour-piercing shells, almost all of which had been expended by both panzers and assault guns in containing the Soviet assault. Nor did it go amiss that the StuGs involved in the battle had defeated nearly 70 tanks in a few hours, the bulk of which had been eliminated by the 1st Batterie of the Abteilung.

One day later the StuGs were employed in their designed role as infantry support when they assisted Infanterie-Regiment 49 to penetrate

BELOW Many Russian bridges that had not been blown up were not strong enough to take the weight of a loaded StuG, which led to what is seen in this picture. The StuG awaits recovery.

LEFT A heavily weighed down assault gun of StuGAbt 177 passes through a Russian village in the opening months of the invasion.

the bunkers of the Stalin Line at Sopockinin. Thereafter, the battalion was deployed to assist other infantry units as and when the need demanded. On 28 June it was assisting the 28th Infanterie Division and on 7 July it found itself operating with the 18th Infanterie Division and crossing the river Düna via a pontoon bridge. Throughout July the battalion advanced eastward, engaging the enemy in a number of encounters and by force of circumstance acting in the role of de facto panzer units and advancing ahead of those infantry formations it was nominally attached to. For example, on the evening of 20 July the 3rd Batterie succeeded in destroying a Russian artillery battery, and along with Infanterie-Regiment 51 captured a village, destroying a large Red Army ammunition dump at the Lomonossovo railway station.

By this date the battalion was operating as part of the northern pincer of Hoth's Panzergruppe, working to encircle large numbers of Red Army forces in the Smolensk pocket in tandem with Guderian's Panzergruppe that was providing the other pincer, coming up from the south of the city. Fighting was understandably extremely heavy. On 9 August the battalion incurred its first total loss when a StuG ran on to a mine and had to abandon the machine, whereupon it was utterly destroyed by Soviet artillery.

After a few days' rest, the Abteilung was attached to the 102nd Infanterie Division.

Soviet forces trapped in the Smolensk pocket were intent on breaking out of the cordon and making heavy attacks on the German forces that were manning the encirclement. The StuGs continued to advance towards Velikiye-Luki, under frequent attack from the Red Air Force – the Luftwaffe no longer being able to operate, as in the first few days of

BELOW 'Mackensen', a StuG from StuGAbt 177.

RIGHT **Where bridges were not available and wherever possible, rivers would be forded.**

the invasion, in conditions of air superiority. Declining resources and losses were reducing its capacity to respond to almost constant calls for assistance – a reality also being experienced by all Sturmgeschütz formations – operating now across an ever widening front.

On 25 August a determined attempt by Soviet forces saw them try to break out of the pocket at Velikiye-Luki and StuGAbt 184 found itself involved in ferocious fighting, resulting in the blunting of the

Russian forces. Thirty-nine enemy trucks were destroyed in the process as well as light tanks. One StuG was destroyed by a direct hit from a Soviet bomber. Continuing its operations with the 102nd Infanterie Division, the StuGAbt continued the advance, acting as the point formation leading to the capture of the town of Toropets. There a halt was called and a short period for rehabilitation of the unit began. This was in no way a major overhaul, but one wherein the surviving machines

BELOW **Two StuGs of StuGAbt 177 take a break from combat within the environs of a typical Russian village.**

LEFT Although a posed picture for the benefit of the Propaganda Kompanie photographer that seems to have been attached to StuGAbt 177, the image is good for the detail that can be seen. 'Seydlitz' was one of the names of the StuGs in the Abteilung – in this case the name of the famous cavalry commander of Frederik the Great's Army. Late summer 1941.

had their engines attended to. The StuGs, as with the panzers, were experiencing many problems associated with the ingestion of the very fine dust that was raised from the 'roads' and clogged air filters and entered the engines, thereby causing breakdowns. Nor was it possible to obtain the necessary spares, as supply lines were stretched and many columns bringing these forward were attacked by Soviet units still at large behind the lines.

Nevertheless, operations resumed, but on 12 September a StuG was immobilised by a direct hit from a surprise Soviet artillery barrage. Heavy fighting was to continue but on 10 October the unit was pulled out of the line and entrained back to Germany for rest and rebuilding. But the respite would be but temporary: StuGAbt 184 would see service in Russia again within a few months and amid ferocious winter conditions.

LEFT Another named StuG of StuGAbt 177, in this case 'Langemarck', recalling the site of the German attack in 1914. The StuG is heavily weighed down although one wonders why it was necessary to carry a replacement wheel. Of note is the manner in which the crew have rigged up an MG34 before the loader's hatch. The binocular sight used by the assault gun commander can also be seen.

StuGAbt 190 – Army Group South

Sturmgeschütz 190 did not participate in the opening phase of Operation 'Barbarossa', not seeing action there until nearly a month later on 20 July. The reason for this was the formation's lengthier participation in the Greek Campaign, with it only returning to Bucharest in Rumania on 14 June. Although it was intended that this formation be given an overhaul before being committed to the Eastern Campaign, that did not come to pass.

On arrival in the East, StuGAbt 190 was subordinated to Army Group South and attached to the 11th Army. Within a matter of days of going into action two of its three Batterien along with its battalion staff were attached to a Vorausabteilung (Advance Guard Detachment) where their firepower and mobility were employed as surrogate panzers to drive ahead of the main Army formations. Indeed, within a day the StuGs were being utilised as the point of the advancing detachment. Over the next few days the Advance Guard captured a number of major towns and on the evening of 26 July the two Batterien were ensconced on hills either side of the town of Ploskoje. It was here they were subject to a heavy attack by a number of enemy companies. The commander of the StuGs placed one battery on his right flank and the other on his left. It was noteworthy

for the battalion in that they found themselves engaged in their first tank battle from which they emerged victorious – the StuGs having defeated four enemy tanks – the type undisclosed.

Resuming the advance, the StuGs were engaged in ongoing combat following up rapidly on a retreating enemy. On the 30th, having reached the river Bug, they found themselves engaged in very heavy fighting wherein the StuGs had to contend with large numbers of enemy anti-tank guns and artillery. It was only by dint of a flank attack that the artillery batteries were defeated – two 150mm howitzers, four 76.2mm cannons and a number of anti-tank guns were knocked out in this five-hour battle that had begun at 05.00hrs and ended at 10.00hrs. The tempo of the advance resumed in the course of which the battalion captured the following enemy matériél: 84 field wagons, 203 horses, 6 field kitchens, 10 heavy machine guns, 5 x 80mm anti-tank guns, 4 x 105mm cannons and 2 howitzers, at a cost of one StuG incurring minor damage from an artillery strike.

From the end of July through to mid-September the Abteilung was involved in heavy fighting even as the German offensive pushed eastward. The river Dnieper was crossed. Up until 20 September it had fought under the command of XXX Armee-Korps HQ, but on the 22nd it was transferred to the LIV Armee-Korps whereupon it received a different task. It was ordered to support a breakthrough into the Crimean peninsula via the isthmus at Perekop, which the Russians had heavily fortified. Up to this point the Abteilung had destroyed and captured 173 guns, 39 mortars, 122 anti-tank guns, 45 tanks, 265 prime movers, trucks, cars, etc, and had lost 32 officers, NCOs and men. Eight StuGs and five SdKfz 252s and 253s had been destroyed.

The attack on the isthmus began on 24 September at daybreak although it took two days to capture the main Tartar trench. New orders saw the assault guns pulled out of the attack on the Crimea and sent further eastward in short order to the port of Mariupol on the Sea of Azov, where the Russians had made a breakthrough threatening the German position there. The Abteilung was involved in heavy fighting containing the Soviets. It was now October and having dealt with that emergency the StuGs were sent back to the isthmus

where the Red Army had succeeded in halting the German attack. The assault guns were once again attached to a Vorausabteilung, which succeeded in breaking through the Soviet defences. What followed illustrated the degree to which StuGs by dint of circumstance were continuing to be employed as surrogate panzers. Penetrating the Soviet rear the StuGs advanced rapidly into the Crimea:

'. . . always the lead element, it took fully occupied airfields, smashed into the rear of fleeing enemy columns and ten days later,

reached the fortress of Sevastapol. An attempt to seize the port fortress by a coup de main failed with the Russians turning their heavy artillery on the attackers. The Abteilung was pulled back to recuperate but then just before Christmas it was involved in the attempt to capture the fortress. The Eleventh Army, under whose auspices it was now fighting, had since become commanded by General von Manstein. It is here that we will take leave of StuGAbt 190 as the winter began to intrude, and turn our focus to the role played by Sturmgeschütz-Batterie 666.

RIGHT A StuG III Ausf A *of* Sturmbatterie 667 fords a shallow river and attempts to gain traction on the muddy bank.

LEFT The onset of even a heavy rain shower was sufficient to turn a Russian 'road' into a muddy track, which only tracked vehicles had any hope of getting through. This StuG Ausf A belongs to Sturmbatterie 667. It belongs to the third Zug of the Batterie as indicated by the Roman numeral 'III' on the side of the fighting compartment.

BELOW The presence of water obstacles that impeded the advance of the German forces in 1941 has already been commented upon. In this instance a StuG of Sturmbatterie 666 of Army Group North is being taken across a river, clearly too deep to ford, on a floating pontoon bridge strong enough to carry the weight of the StuG.

ABOVE Given the prevalence of swampy terrain in European Russia, the recovery of any vehicle – in this case a StuG of Abt 177 – might need help from a number of tracked or semi-tracked vehicles to help extricate itself. In this case two SdKfz 11, 3-ton half-tracks are seen pulling the StuG, while the half-tracks are in turn being pulled by another machine, out of shot.

RIGHT When time permitted it was possible for some rest and recuperation. Five of the six StuG IIIs of Sturmbatterie 667 and their supporting vehicles take the time to wash and shave, something that given the pace of the German advance in the summer of 1941 they may not have been able to do for some time. The StuGs would also get a wash to get rid of the all-pervading dust, as would the other vehicles – one SdKfz 252 can be seen as well as two 1-ton half-tracks towing ammunition trailers.

LEFT A broken-down StuG III is recovered by an 18-ton half-track and a flatbed. The StuG belongs to Sturmbatterie 666.

ABOVE There were a number of occasions in the opening months of the Russian Campaign when StuGs and panzers found it necessary to halt T-34s and KV-1s by the drastic expedient of ramming them. In this case it was a StuG of Sturmbatterie 666.

ABOVE The crewmen of an SdKfz 253 attend to their responsibilities – spying out the lie of the land and looking for enemy units hiding or operating within it – and reporting back to their StuG commanders. Production of this armoured observation post variant of the standard SdKfz 250 was terminated in June 1941.

BELOW In this photograph taken by a soldier using his personal Leica camera, a StuG of Abteilung 192 is seen advancing warily through a Russian village. Both the StuG and soldiers have thought it necessary to attach pieces of vegetation to their vehicle and helmets as camouflage. StuGAbt 192 employed a very distinctive skull and crossbones as its unit insignia.

ABOVE A StuG is having its engine removed, either for maintenance purposes or to be fitted with a replacement. Engines were never fully overhauled by the unit work companies but sent back to Germany. They were returned overhauled and fully ready to reinstall in a StuG.

RIGHT The 18-ton SdKfz 9 FAMO half-track prime mover was one of the most prized machines in Panzer and StuG units. It was the primary recovery vehicle and always in short supply. Even such a powerful machine as this could get bogged down in the innumerable watercourses that criss-crossed the Russian countryside. 'FAMO' came from Fahrzeug- und Motorenbau GmbH (FAMO) of Breslau, its original builder.

RIGHT A StuG III of Abt 184 lies utterly shattered and abandoned. Destroyed either by a mine or a direct hit from a Russian heavy artillery piece, it is unlikely the crew would have survived such destruction. The hulk would have been stripped of all usable parts and abandoned, to be retrieved in due course perhaps, and sent back to Germany for recycling.

Sturmgeschütz-Batterie 666 – Army Group North

Almost from the outset the forces of Army Group North, tasked with the occupation of the Baltic States and the capture of Leningrad, found themselves fighting both the terrain and the Red Army – with each proving to be equally difficult. Sturmbatterie 666 found this to be the case within hours of its crossing the Russian border. In support of the 32nd Infanterie Division, almost the whole of the StuG unit got bogged down in swampy ground and were recovered using their unit 18-ton half-tracks. Over the next few days the unit advanced, destroying enemy artillery batteries and infantry formations. Its rate of advance soon left the infantry behind and it was recalled, moving back some 26km, with the 1st section dealing with a Russian attack on the divisional right flank. The river Memel was reached but the bridge constructed by the engineers was not strong enough to carry the StuGs, so a diversion of 80km had to be made to cross the stronger bridge at Kovno.

On 29 June the 3rd section was assigned to a Vorausabteilung, which clashed with strong Soviet forces destroying trucks and taking prisoners. In the following days the Batterie found itself engaged in heavy fighting, having to contend with an enemy counter-attack. This was carried out without infantry, with the StuGs

functioning as tanks! In the days following the advance continued but by 2 July losses among the StuGs and other support vehicles had become so great 'that they had to be reorganised' into two sections. By 9 July the StuGs and the infantry they were supporting were butting up against the fortifications of the Stalin Line. One assault gun crossed a river by a ford and assaulted the enemy positions, rolling them up one by one – doing exactly the sort of job the StuG had been designed for.

The advance continued with the same targets – hidden enemy positions, fortified villages, bunkers and units of the enemy coming out of the very thick forests flanking the sandy tracks that passed for roads. On 16 July the Batterie captured two bridges from the enemy, which led to very heavy fighting over the course of the next few days. One StuG took a direct hit from a 76.2mm gun – the shell got stuck in the armour. Another transfer to assist the 407th Infanterie Regiment took place on 19 July, which was attempting to take a town called Krasnoye. The attack began at 14.00hrs with the 1st and 2nd Sections overpowering the enemy's positions, but as the Batterie continued to advance 'through thick forested cover, it ran up into heavy fire from artillery and anti-tank guns'. A Soviet counter-attack was thrown back. It was on this day that the battery suffered its first KIA. The date of 24 July saw the Batterie transferred again

BELOW Three StuGs speed across the terrain for the likely benefit of a PK (Propaganda Kompanie) photographer. The terrain is redolent of that fought through by Army Group North in its advance on Leningrad.

– this time to assist in the attack towards Cholm. Some days later Senior HQ ordered the battery to move to the west of Lake Ilmen – a march of 380km from their previous position which, unsurprisingly, led to breakdowns. Indeed, by 8 August the Batterie had only three combat-ready StuGs available. A section from StuG Batterie was attached to bring 666 back to strength.

The advance northward continued. On 10 August it crossed the river Mschaga and fought its way in the direction of Korostym. Assistance with the attack on Novgorod was not possible by virtue of the available bridge being unable to take the weight of the StuGs, and Batterie 659 was reurned to its parent formation on the same day, thereby reducing the strength of 666. The last two weeks in August saw the Batterie assisting in the thrust towards Leningrad. In this operation it was attached to the 18th Motorised Infantry Division. In the next few days a number of Russian tanks were destroyed and on the 28th came yet another order to transfer to the II Armee-Korps in Cholm. What was not an appreciably long distance to travel turned into over a week of struggling along sand roads, which then turned into morasses with the onset of a heavy rain storm. The Batterie did not reach its objective until 8 September.

Following a hiatus in combat lasting most of September, the Batterie next saw combat on 9 October helping to clear enemy positions amid

forest, assisting 12th Infanterie Division. The operation proved expensive – in the following three days three StuGs were lost to mines – one of which was a total write-off. The depleted formation continued in combat but 17 October was to prove another expensive day. Ordered to support the attack of an Infanterie Regiment of a bunker line supported by machine-gun nests, the 1st Section advanced followed by the command StuG, which then ran on to a mine and was heavily damaged. A 252 ammunition carrier also ran on to a mine and was a total loss. Unsurprisingly the attack foundered. Pulling back, the surviving StuGs fired on the enemy positions but then came under very

ABOVE A StuG III of Abt 659 is given the 'once over' by two interested soldiers.

LEFT 'Prinz Eugen' – having forded the river a StuG III has become firmly mired in the mud on the bank. Three Russian POWs have been impressed (or volunteered) to assist in digging out the StuG. Tree trunks have been collected in a pile in preparation for placing beneath the tracks to give them purchase once the StuG has been dug free of the mud. The first snow has fallen and winter is coming.

heavy artillery fire, forcing the StuGs to pull back out of range leaving the two knocked-out machines to be captured by the enemy. The following day saw yet another StuG lost to mines in consequence of which the formation was pulled back behind the lines with now just three StuGs remaining.

At the end of December the Batterie was deployed in the Staraya Russa area. However, the operations of the StuG formations is not of concern – suffice it to say both StuG crews and machines suffered from the same privations experienced by all German troops during the winter of 1941/42.

There is no question, that if the verdict on the StuG was favourable even before the start of 'Barbarossa', the performance of the Sturmartillerie between June and December 1941 in the East was adjudged outstanding. Of the total committed to the invasion 96 had been lost by the end of 1941.

Prelude to the expansion of the assault gun arm

The half year of combat on the Eastern Front had proved more of a real blooding for the Sturmartillerie than either of the previous campaigns and it demonstrated overwhelmingly the efficacy of the assault gun concept. Increasingly, by virtue of the sheer number of Russian machines that were encountered relative to the much smaller number of German panzers, the StuG formations had perforce become increasingly employed not only as tank destroyers but even as substitute tank units. Such was recognised in a meeting involving Hitler and senior representatives of the armaments industries towards the end of November 1941 to discuss production priorities for the following year. It was noted that:

'. . . the objective must be to assign tanks to the motorised divisions, providing them with an armoured spearhead, thereby releasing *the assault guns that are currently being used for that purpose* [author's italic]'.

The actual purpose for which the assault gun had been originally designed was reinforced:

'Assault vehicles belong with the infantry whom they must escort directly.'

It was also noted, and as we have seen, it was Hitler who insisted that:

'Assault vehicles must be fitted with a gun that is highly effective against tanks [viz, T-34 and KV series]. The assault guns must be provided with more ammunition.'

Contrary, therefore, to the observation quoted above that assault guns must stay with infantry, the reality of equipping the StuG with a more powerful weapon (initially the 75mm StuK 40 L/43, and then the L/48) meant that it would become in 1942, alongside the similarly armed up-gunned Panzer IV F/2 and model G, the most powerful mobile anti-armour weapon on the battlefield. It would thus necessarily continue to be employed as a tank destroyer and even when circumstances required – as a substitute tank.

Although the Panzer III, the primary medium tank of the panzer divisions, had finally been up-gunned with an L/60 50mm weapon in the Ausf J, which went into production in December 1941, it was still unable to penetrate the frontal armour of either Soviet tank at battle ranges. Nor was its turret ring large enough to take the 75mm KwK L/48 main gun as was being fitted to the Panzer IV and the StuG. Its days as a battle tank were thus numbered, with its replacement in the form of the much heavier and more powerful Panther medium tank already projected by the end of 1942. But as we have seen in earlier chapters, the chassis of the Mk III, suitably modified for use on the assault gun, would come to be used solely for that purpose through to the end of the conflict.

The assault gun had generated for itself a formidable reputation at the front by virtue of its ability to take on and defeat the heavier Soviet tanks. This was not because it was better armed, as it was equipped with the same weapon as the Panzer IV – the 75mm L/24. What had helped the StuG was its very low height, making it difficult for Russian tanks to hit, and if fighting on the defensive, easier to hide under cover. Furthermore, its relatively heavy frontal armour was also an asset. Such was the impression made on the Red Army by the performance of the assault gun battalions that they became the only other combatant of the war to embark on a programme to build their own version of a StuG, initially in the form of the SU-122. However, it would be some while before this Russian type appeared on the battlefield.

Numbers of the L/24-equipped StuG peaked in December 1941 with 625 on strength, though a total of 96 had been lost between June and December. Production of the short-barrelled StuG in December 1941 was 46, 45 in January and 45 in February 1942. The last of this type left the production line in that month. In March the numbers of StuGs produced plummeted as Alkett, still at this stage of the conflict the

sole producer of the assault gun, tooled up to begin production of the L/43-armed Ausf F, in consequence of which just three were built. By April, the numbers leaving the production line had risen, reaching 36, and then one month later in May, to 79.

Such had been the German losses in manpower and matériél in the 1941 campaign, a resumption of the offensive in Russia along three fronts was out of the question. Hitler therefore determined to attack on only one sector, that being in the south of Russia, with the ultimate objective being the capture of the oilfields in the Caucasus, which if realised he was convinced would force the USSR to surrender. But before the summer campaign in the south began, the Soviets launched a major offensive in early May 1942 designed to recapture the city of Kharkov. Even though there were large numbers of T-34s and KV-1s employed by the Russians in this offensive, it failed, being seen down by superior German mobility and tactics. Of note was the role played by StuG units. A report by StuGAbt 244 after the battle provides interesting statistics and observations:

'Between 13 May and 14 June the StuGAbt destroyed or captured 100 enemy medium and heavy tanks and a further 86 in the final encirclement battle. The German unit in turn lost 5 StuGs over that same period. It should be noted that these losses were inflicted on the enemy even though the StuG always had to fire within the range of the 76.2mm main gun of the T-34 and KV-1. There were, of course, other losses among support vehicles and also breakdowns, the latter of which included 18 StuGs. Other losses from among the participating panzer divisions and other StuG Abteilungen ran to 5 and 18 respectively, of which 50 per cent of the latter could be repaired.'

It is apparent that Soviet tankers had acquired a very healthy respect for StuG units as on more than one occasion even the appearance of the assault guns was sufficient to prompt the attackers to turn away. The captured commander of the 148th Tank Brigade stated to his captors that '. . . his brigade had been heavily attacked by Sturmgeschütz. The enemy considers our combat tactics more agile and our weaponry more precise.'

There is no question that the performance

of the short L/24 on the StuGs was enhanced by the first employment of the new Panzer-Sprenggranate 38 shaped-charge shell during the operation to defeat the Soviet offensive at Kharkov. It was noted that this ammunition performed best when employed between 300 and 700m range. The report noted that: 'The round must have a true penetrating ability, leaving only a small hole of 2 to 3cm diameter in the armour. Inside the tank, the very high heat it generated ignited everything within a short time.' While this new ammunition offered a short-term aide to the problem of coping with the T-34 and KV-1, it was long apparent that the 75mm L/24 was not up to the task of defeating these premier Red Army tanks. Hence the need to up-gun the StuG with a weapon that could defeat them far more easily.

Enter the long-barrelled Sturmgeschütz

It fell to the Infanterie Regiment Grossdeutschland, albeit raised to the status of a division on 1 April 1942, to first see action with the new StuG Ausf F armed with the L/43 main gun. As we have seen, the organic StuG Batterie that GD had employed since May 1940 had come about via the permanent attachment of what was originally SturmgeschützBatterie

640 to the regiment, whereupon it had been redesignated 16.(StuG.)/I.R.(mot) GD. With the rebuilding of GD in Germany after it had been decimated in Russia in early 1942, its StuG Batterie was raised to the level of an Abteilung by being merged with StuGAbt 192.

Having returned to Russia, GD was earmarked for employment in 'Case Blue', the German offensive in southern Russia. By June 1942 there were 19 Sturmgeschützen Abteilungen – including that of GD – and one Batterie serving on the Eastern Front. In the same manner that the OKH had 'stripped' panzer divisions serving with Army Groups North and Centre to reinforce those committed to 'Blue', no fewer than 13 StuGAbt were earmarked to serve with Army Group South, leaving just six StuGAbt serving with the other two Army Groups. Most of the early deliveries of the StuG Ausf F and then the F/8 were prioritised for service with Army Group South in the forthcoming offensive and as replacements once it began.

As part of the 48th Panzer Corps, the newly reconstituted and rebuilt GD division was deployed on the extreme left wing of Army Group South, when the summer offensive began on 28 June 1942. It was here that the new Langrohr StuG first saw combat. An after-

RIGHT The new long-barrelled assault gun is clearly of great interest both to the German officers being given a viewing of the new machine by its crew and also to the young Russian lads looking on.

action report was completed that covered operations with the newly armed assault gun through to 7 July, a number of observations from which are given here. Having listed the number of rounds and the type that had been fired, it noted that a direct hit with an HE round could be achieved up to 800m. This was followed by stating that:

'. . . the impact of the new PzGr 39 was surprisingly good. All Russian tanks including the KV-1 were clearly penetrated at 600m. Even the T-34, the hardest tank to defeat, was destroyed by clear penetrations, despite having sloped armour on the front, turret and sides . . . during the period 28 June and 7 July, the Abteilung destroyed 41 tanks of all types.'

While the report pointed to the clear capacity of the Langrohr, with the same weapon being employed on the Panzer IV F2 – to neutralise the former ability of the T-34 and KV-1 to withstand German tank guns and PaK anti-tank weapons – in June 1942 it was still the case that the bulk of StuGs on the Eastern Front were equipped with the short-barrelled 75mm L/24. It would not be until the end of 1942, by which time the Ausf F/8 with the 75mm L/48, was in production and equipping StuG

formations, that the actual balance of L/24-equipped StuGs relative to L/43/48-equipped StuGs, would be resolved in favour of the latter weapons.

This is reflected in the content of a document issued by the General Staff of the Army dated April 1943, that drew attention to the increasing number of StuG Abteilungen being created:

'. . . in the second half of 1942, the number of StuG units has increased by 150 per cent, while the total number of vehicles available had increased by 210 per cent. This was a result of progress with re-organisation. In early 1942, all StuG Abteilung at the front were still authorised to have six or seven StuGs per battery. All newly established units or those refurbished during the autumn/winter were brought up to ten StuGs per battery. Over this period, a total of 510 Sturmgeschütz were written off as total losses, while 659 were received as replacements.'

Even though, throughout 1942, Alkett was still the only producer of the Sturmgeschütz III, the numbers of the L/43 and L/48 models had increased such that whereas there were 18 StuG Abteilungen at the beginning of the year with all of these being equipped with the L/24 weapon, by its end a further ten StuGAbt had

ABOVE A StuG III Ausf F/8 of Abt 177 in 1942. It is painted dark grey, the standard finish on German AFVs in Russia until 1943.

been raised. Most of the new formations had received the long-barrelled StuGs, but those of earlier foundation received the Langrohr StuG as replacements for Kurzrohr StuGs that had been lost. They were a mixed establishment. Whereas at the beginning of 1942 there were 166 StuGs ready for combat, with a further 44 in the workshops under repair, at year's end there were 315 combat ready and 127 under repair.

New StuG Abteilungen raised in 1942	
Number of StuG Abt	Month of establishment in 1942
249	January
600	March
667	June
287	August
228	November
232	November
242	November
270	December
904	December
905	December

All of these newly raised StuGAbt were destined for service in the East. It was only with the Allied invasion of Sicily in July 1943, the landings at Salerno in September and Italy's subsequent exit from the war, that StuG Abteilungen were despatched to that new theatre of war. Four StuG Abteilungen were destroyed at Stalingrad, namely Nos 177, 243, 244 and 245 with a total of 106 StuGs and 8 assault howitzers being lost together with their crews. These formations were, however, re-established by March 1943 and equipped with the new Ausf G model. They were then returned to serve in the East.

It was in consequence of the grandiosely named 'Adolf Hitler Tank Programme' of September 1942 that the production targets for German armour were set down. It envisaged a huge rise in output from the German perspective from the total of 445 tanks and assault gun/tank destroyers produced in that month, to no fewer than 1,200 per month by the end of 1944. This number also embraced a qualitative change with the targeted number of 800 panzers including 600 Panthers (of which production would not begin until 1943) and 50 Tigers, with the latter just beginning to leave the production line at Henschel. The other 400 were pencilled in as assault guns and tank destroyers. However, by the winter of 1942/43 with the defeat of the German Sixth Army at Stalingrad, and the losses incurred in the subsequent ferocious winter fighting, panzer numbers in the Ostheer began to decline rapidly. By March 1943 there were only 1,686 on strength of which just 895 were operational.

It is hardly surprising, given the

RIGHT A Japanese military attaché on an inspection tour observes a StuG III Ausf F/8 passing. The camouflage scheme could place this image to the spring of 1943, although some StuGs were finished in the colours used in the North African theatre in 1942. Note that the officer accompanying the Japanese attaché is Luftwaffe. The Luftwaffe eagle on the helmet of the furthermost crewman suggests this could be a StuG from a Luftwaffe field unit.

LEFT The StuG III F/8 in the background is fitted with the *Winterketten* or 'winter tracks'. This widened the track to lower the StuG's ground pressure in the snow and stop it from sinking. After the SdKfz 252's replacement as an ammunition resupply vehicle, surviving machines were also employed as extemporised command vehicles. Winter 1942/43.

circumstances and the perceived effectiveness of the Sturmgeschütz as a highly effective tank destroyer, allied to its cheaper and easier build relative to that of the panzers in production (of which not enough could be produced to replace losses) that the assault gun was seen as both an effective and economically more desirable substitute. February 1943 had also seen the firm of MIAG become the second source for the production of the StuG. What is more, in December 1942 a new model, the Ausf G (a reworked Ausf F with a new and larger fighting compartment married to the 75mm StuK L/48) entered production. Some 120 were produced in December 1942 by Alkett. MIAG did not begin to see the numbers it produced of this model rise to over 50 until March 1943. Thereafter its output

LEFT A StuG III F/8 that has seen a lot of action. It is equipped with *Winterketten* and was serving with StuGAbt 901 during the winter of 1942/43.

increased such that the combined output of the StuG Ausf G during 1943 reached a total of 3,011 machines when compared to the 702 produced by Alkett alone in 1942.

Such numbers presaged yet another expansion of the Sturmartillerie and the employment of the assault gun by other, new operators, who coveted its formidable reputation as a tank destroyer and capacity to be used as a surrogate panzer. The table on page 132 detailing Sturmartillerie status from June through to December 1942 illustrates just how important the StuG units were becoming in the OstHeer's Order of Battle. As of June 1942 there were 18 StuG Abteilungen operating in the East with a total of 210 StuGs on strength, of which 166 were combat ready with the remainder under repair, seven months later the figures had changed markedly. As of 28 December 1942 there was now 27 StuG Abteilungen operating on the Eastern Front fielding a grand total of 442 machines, of which 315 were combat ready with 127 under repair. This rising trajectory of StuG units and numbers would increase substantially in 1943 with the onset of Sturmgeschütz Ausf G and mass-production of the assault gun saw it acquiring a much more important role in the Wehrmacht.

BELOW The last German offensive success in Russia was the operation to recapture Kharkov in the late winter of 1942/43. Although still classified as a Panzer Grenadier Division the 1st Waffen SS Division LAH (Leibstandarte Adolf Hitler) was equipped with its own StuG III Ausf G Abteilung. This unit received the latest and last variant of the StuG in early 1943 when it was re-formed in France before returning to Russia.

1943 – year of the StuG?

The return to Russia from France of the three units that comprised the newly formed II SS Panzer Korps in early 1943 provided Field Marshal von Manstein with a powerful force with which to launch a counter-offensive against the overextended and weakening Red Army forces that had captured Kharkov. Although the three SS formations – namely the Leibstandarte SS Adolf Hitler, Das Reich and Totenkopf – had been rebuilt as fully-fledged divisions, they were classified as Panzer-Grenadier and not Panzer Divisions, although their armoured complement was large enough for them to have been designated as such. Although all three had fielded a Sturmbatterie as part of the expansion process, each of their establishments now comprised a fully-fledged Abteilung, which was operated primarily in the role of tank destroyers. GD was also part of the force employed by Manstein to defeat the Soviet forces at Kharkov. Between 7 and 20 March 1943 the division claimed 230 T-34s, 16 T-60s or 70s, and 3 KV-1s destroyed. Of these the 35 StuGs of the division accounted for 41 – all by assault guns mounting the long L/48 main gun.

Nor would these three SS formations be

the only units to benefit from the allocation of assault guns. The general expansion of the Waffen SS in the last two years of the war would see many more StuGs entering service with newly constituted SS divisions. By the time of the Allied invasion of Normandy in June 1944, and the subsequent campaign there, many of the SS divisions that were sent to fight in that theatre were fielding StuGs – in some cases as we shall see, in lieu of panzers. However, by the beginning of 1943 it was not just the SS that was seeing the acquisition of assault guns.

If the infantry and artillery looked askance at the diversion of assault guns to service other arms at their expense, the formation of Luftwaffe field units in mid-1942 to which new-build assault guns were also diverted, must have left them feeling apoplectic. It was, however, indicative of the chaotic thinking of the Nazi hierarchy that the need to equip these Luftwaffe units saw equipment such as StuGs hived off to provide for these at a time when the panzer divisions and StuG Abteilungen in the east were in such a dire state and in need of re-equipment. At first just 4 StuGs were allocated to each Luftwaffe field unit but this figure was raised in 1944 to 10 StuGs. However, the formation of two Luftwaffe Sturmgeschütz Brigaden saw each equipped with a full Abteilung equipped with 32 StuGs. Much of the equipment supplied was frittered away as the Luftwaffe formations were to prove ineffective and poorly led and made little contribution to supporting the Army.

Nor did the diversion of assault guns away from their original role stop there. The irony of the matter was that it was down to the appointment of Heinz Guderian – the long-time opponent of the assault artillery concept – as Inspector General of Armoured Troops by Hitler in early 1943, that saw the StuG enter service in the panzer divisions. Thomas Anderson succinctly accounts for this reversal of conviction as follows:

'. . . around March/April 1943, the Generalinspekteur der Panzertruppe decreed that the three tank divisions (14, 16 and 24 Pz Div) lost at Stalingrad were to be re-established. Beside the standard I.Abt and II.Abt, all the divisions were authorised

ABOVE A StuG III F/8 of the Hermann Goering Division in Sicily in July 1943, at the time of the Allied invasion of the island. They have already applied vegetation as camouflage in a bid to hide themselves from Allied fighter-bombers.

to form a III.Abt (Sturmgeschütz). Guderian, who had vehemently opposed the large-scale introduction of the Sturmgeschütz from the beginning, had finally to accept out of sheer necessity. In 1943, German tank production was barely able to replace the heavy and continuous tank losses and at the same time satisfy the requirements for the establishment of new units. Only the manufacturers of the Sturmgeschütz would prove to be capable of significantly increasing production.' (See graph of StuG production overleaf.)

While the Adolf Hitler Tank Programme had toyed with the idea of abandoning the production of the Panzer IV, Guderian was absolutely insistent that it be kept in production. But as the numbers being built could not be increased, it became necessary to utilise the StuG where, as we have seen, production from the beginning of 1943 began to rise

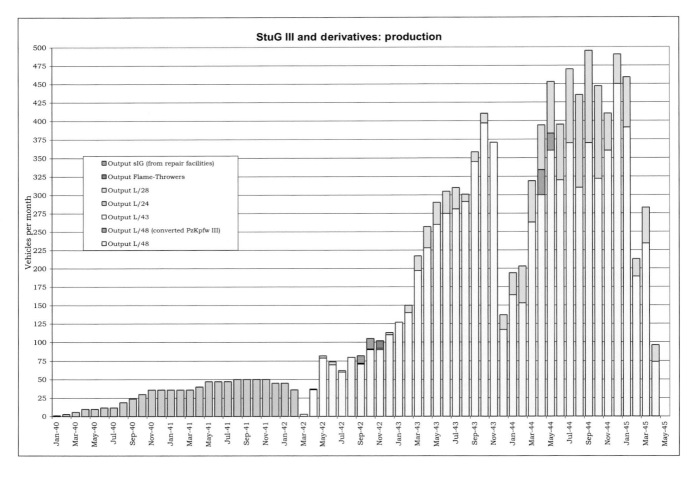

StuG III and derivatives: production

Legend:
- □ Output sIG (from repair facilities)
- ■ Output Flame-Throwers
- □ Output L/28
- □ Output L/24
- □ Output L/43
- ■ Output L/48 (converted PzKpfw III)
- □ Output L/48

Y-axis: Vehicles per month

BELOW Although the image dates from mid-1943 at the Alkett works in Berlin, the introduction of the Ausf G in December for Alkett, and February 1943 with MIAG, saw a great expansion of the production of the assault gun. The Ausf G would remain in production through to the end of the conflict with the two companies producing between them 8,416 assault guns armed with the 75 StuK 40 L/48 main gun.

substantially as a substitute. But he was at pains to stress in an Instructional Document of 3 June 1943, which addressed the role of the StuG within a Panzer Regiment, that: 'Some PzDiv will be *temporarily* issued with Sturmgeschütz as an interim solution.'

Such was his intention, but as the conflict turned against Germany and the need for ever more AFVs increased, the StuG never ceased to serve in some number or other with the panzer divisions. He recognised that the StuG did have a number of advantages vis-à-vis a panzer: it had a low height resulting in the presentation of a small target to the enemy and initially it had heavier frontal armour to the Panzer IV (this was increased on the latter). However, to his mind, the disadvantages of the type were greater. It lacked the all-important facility of fully traversable turret and all-round fire. Close defence of the StuG was impaired by its lack of a machine gun with all-round fire. Due to its performance and characteristics the StuG could not be deployed independently without the assistance of panzer or Panzer Grenadiers to protect its vulnerable flanks. It had merit, though, as a tank destroyer and that dictated the manner of its employment, and thus when attacking it would be in the last wave. When operating as tank destroyers the StuGs would follow the 'open' side of the PzAbt when engaging enemy tanks. It was then in a tank destroyer role that Guderian saw the StuG being used by the PzAbt and not as a surrogate tank. Nonetheless, it was not the case that these injunctions were always adhered to.

Guderian was able to secure at least 100 of the total number of StuGs produced each month. Specifically, those panzer divisions initially concerned – the 14th, 16th and 24th – had been destroyed at Stalingrad and which in April 1943 had been ordered rebuilt by Guderian. Initially it was envisaged that they would be of three regiments – the first of Panthers, the second of Panzer IVs and the third of assault guns. In each case there were to be 96 of each machine to each regiment. It did not happen.

March 1943 also saw the 105mm HH 18-armed Sturmhaubitze enter production at Alkett. Indeed, this company would alone produce 1,299 of this variant of the StuG with the last being manufactured in April 1945. The concept of this new variant had been tested with the nine pre-production machines built using reconditioned Panzer III chassis in combat with Army Group North, although that which entered production at Alkett in March 1943 was based on the Ausf G. The primary impact of the introduction of the new variant was the way it changed the make-up of the standard StuG Batterie, with this now comprising seven 75mm StuK L/48 and three 105mm StuH, although this composition was not rigid. A unit commander could vary the numbers of the two types if he was of the view that the task in hand merited that change. It was also understood that the new StuH would only ever attempt to fight an enemy tank as a last resort.

With the onset of the third year of the war in Russia, steps were being taken to rehabilitate German mobile formations in the East and the role of the Sturmgeschütze would acquire ever greater significance. In the early spring of 1943 a detailed tally of the numbers of assault guns in the East yielded the following information:

Sturmgeschütz availability as at 14 April 1943							
Army Group	StuG Abt	Stug Bty	Unit status	StuG status	Short barrel	Long barrel	StuH
North	912		Unit in delivery	CR in work		22	9
	184			CR in work	8 3	9 6	
	226			CR in work		13 15	
Centre	177		Unit in delivery	CR in work		22	
	202			CR in work	7 2	10 3	
	904			CR in work		13 6	
	189			CR in work		20 2	
	270			CR in work	6 3	17	
	667			CR in work	4 2	11 4	
	185			CR in Work		11 1	5
South	203			CR in work		4 23	
	210			CR in work		14 3	
	243			CR		31	
		287		CR		3	
	209			CR in work		7 2	
	232			CR in work		6 3	
		Lehr 901		CR in work		6	
	911			CR in Work		22	
	228			CR in work		9 8	
	'GD'			CR in work		19 13	
	A	249		CR in work	7 1	10	
	191			CR in work		8	
West	905			CR in work		20 2	
Afrika		1/242		CR in work		4	
Total					43	402	14

CR = combat ready
in work = in workshop

of tanks'. That, however, was not to be as a series of factors came into play that saw the launch date set back by two months. When finally the offensive was launched on 4/5 July 1943, Hitler's stated prerequisite that it must be assured of surprise had vanished as the Soviets waited behind immense defences, having amassed the largest armoured reserve the Red Army would ever assemble in the course of the conflict.

The Battle of Kursk

The German offensive of 1943 was directed at the elimination of the very large Russian salient centred on the city of Kursk in eastern Ukraine. The intention was to eliminate it by a concentric assault from the north and south and destroy the encircled Red Army units within. It was hoped thereby to blunt any further Soviet offensive efforts for the rest of the summer. This was to be a forlorn hope as the Red Army, aware some time in advance of German intentions, had transformed the salient into one huge defensive bastion protected by massive

ABOVE An Alkett publicity shot taken in March 1943 when the first Sturmhaubitze SdKfz 142/3 left the production line. The company would eventually produce 1,299 before the end of the war.

The reinforcement of those armoured formations destined to serve in the forthcoming summer offensive in Russia began to take absolute priority from early 1943. New-build panzers and StuGs flowed eastward to bolster the forces of Army Groups Centre and South. As originally envisaged with Operation 'Citadel', Hitler insisted that the offensive should begin 'as soon as the ground was dry to allow for the operation

RIGHT MIAG also took publicity shots of new machines they were building, in this case the Sturmgeschütz III Ausf G that first left their production lines in February 1943. By the end of the war they had constructed 2,643 of these assault guns.

minefields and fortified defensive lines built astride the northern and southern necks of the bulge where the German forces were planning to strike.

When finally launched on 5 July, the German Army was fielding a total of 2,795 tanks and other armoured vehicles. These included some of their most up-to-date tanks including Tiger Is, Panthers (its combat debut) and Ferdinand heavy tank destroyers. However, the most numerous tanks were the Panzer III (its swansong as a battle tank) and the Panzer IV. The third largest number of AFVs was of the Sturmgeschütz, of which a total of 466 were committed to the operation. This was of the total of 745 StuG IIIs and 68 StuHs on strength as of 1 July, four days before the launch of Operation 'Citadel'.

The two tables below account for the StuGs and StuHs employed in the battle.

ABOVE The introduction of *Schürzen*, 5mm sheet metal skirts on the StuG III in the spring of 1943, was to protect it from the 14.5mm anti-tank rifles used in their thousands by Russian infantry. Most but not all StuGs were fitted with these in time for the Battle of Kursk.

Independent StuG Abteilungen at Kursk, 4 July 1943				
StuG Abt	Army area deployed in	Corps subordinated to	Number of StuG	Number of StuH
177	9th	XLI Pz Korps	22	9
185	9th	XXIII Pz Korps	27	5
189	9th	XXIII Pz Korps	31	0
202	2nd		31*	0
228	Kempf	III Pz Korps	31	0
244	9th	XLI Pz Korps	22	9
245	9th	XLVII Pz Korps	22	9
904	9th	XLVII Pz Korps	31	0
905	Kempf	Raus	23**	9
909	9th	XLVI Pz Korps	22	9
911	4th Pz Army	XLVIII Pz Korps	22	9
393rd Batterie	Kempf	Raus	12	0

* incl 7 kurz L/24   ** = incl 4 kurz L/24

There were, in addition, the following StuG Abteilungen organic to the following divisions.

StuG Abt	Army area deployed in	Corps subordinated to	Number of StuG	Number of StuH
Grossdeutschland	4th Pz Armee	XLVIII Pz Korps	35	0
1st SS LAH	4th Pz Armee	II SS Pz Korps	35	0
2nd SS Das Reich	4th Pz Armee	II SS Pz Korps	34	0
3rd SS Totenkopf	4th Pz Armee	II SS Pz Korps	35	0

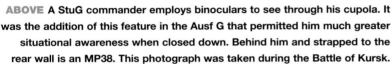

ABOVE A StuG commander employs binoculars to see through his cupola. It was the addition of this feature in the Ausf G that permitted him much greater situational awareness when closed down. Behind him and strapped to the rear wall is an MP38. This photograph was taken during the Battle of Kursk.

ABOVE RIGHT A StuH with its crew taking a break. They may yet join combat as the gun has a cover over the muzzle brake.

BELOW The Battle of Kursk marked the operational debut of the first of the Red Army's heavy self-propelled guns in the form of the SU-152. Based upon the KV chassis, it mounted a 152mm gun in a fixed mounting much like the StuG III. It was the first of a whole tranche of machines that appeared in 1944 such as the ISU-122 and ISU-152 built on the chassis of the IS-II.

Most, but certainly not all, of the StuGs committed to the Kursk offensive now wore 5mm-thick *Schürzen*. These were skirts attached to the sides of the StuG (and also on the Panzer III and IV) to provide a measure of stand-off protection against the mass of 14.5mm anti-tank rifles deployed by Soviet infantry, which had the ability to penetrate the side armour of the assault guns. New-build StuGs left the factories already equipped with these – especially those earmarked for service at Kursk – while in May, 350 sets of *Schürzen* were sent eastward to ensure that the StuGs already in theatre and intended for the offensive would be so fitted when it began.

LEFT A StuG III camouflaged in sand yellow and green is seen engaging in what the assault gun had gained a great reputation for – taking out Russian armour at quite long range. The year 1943 marked the pinnacle of the StuG's fighting effectiveness as in 1944 the Red Army began to make major improvements in the effectiveness of the armour it was fielding (see text). It was nonetheless, in conditions such as these, on the treeless steppe-lands of southern Russia that the StuG garnered its greatest tally of Soviet armour.

STUG FUNKLENK UNITS

The elimination of minefields had called forth a number of solutions from the combatant nations in the Second World War. The main one employed by the German Army was novel. Its basis was the use of a remotely controlled tracked vehicle to deposit a large charge near or in the minefield to be eliminated. The vehicle itself was not crewed at this point, being under remote control from a command vehicle, with the Sturmgeschütz III being one of them executing that task in the Kursk offensive. The Borgward B IV radio-controlled vehicle was normally driven by one man when not in combat.

The Borgward Company had developed a number of models running from 1 through to 3 before the Waffenamt, having evaluated a number of these in the mine-clearing role at the beginning of the Russian Campaign, issued a contract in October 1941 for the development of a radio-controlled vehicle to carry a demolition charge. The machine Borgward designed received the designation Borgward B IV (SdKfz 301), with the first prototype emerging in March 1942.

A 500kg Sprengladung was carried by the B IV and deposited at the designated position. The charge itself was retained on the tracked chassis at the front of the machine by two swing arms. Under remote

StuG-led Funklenk units operating between spring 1943 and May 1945	
StuG (Funklenk) unit	**Sturmgeschütz model**
311	Ausf G
312	Ausf G
314	Ausf G
315	Ausf G
316	Ausf G
317	Ausf G
319	Ausf G
301	Ausf G
302	Ausf G
Funklenk-Panzerzug/Panzer Abteilung (Funklenk) 303	Ausf G

instruction these arms were raised, resulting in the charge sliding down the front of the angled glacis of the B IV.

Panzer-Kompanie (Fkl) 312 operated at Kursk in the sector of Ninth Army, Army Group Centre, under the operational control of Panzer-Brigade 21. It was used to breach the minefields in front of the heavily defended town of Maloarchangelsk. After Kursk, the Funklenk units continued to serve, being present in Normandy and operating also with the Panzer III and Tiger I and II as command vehicles to the end of the conflict.

ABOVE Although Kursk did not result in the huge losses in panzers and assault guns that were thought to have been the case for many years, there were indeed the inevitable losses. In this image two StuG III Ausf Gs are being examined by repair crews to see if it is possible to cannibalise spare parts. Otherwise these two vehicles are total write-offs.

The duration of the battle was not long but it was a decisive clash. Initial operations began on 4 July with the main offensive in the north and south of the salient beginning the following day. The StuG battalions served in their classic role as infantry support as well as tank destroyers.

Hitler finally called off all offensive operations on 17 July as Soviet counter-offensives had begun in the rear of German Ninth Army in the north of the salient and many miles to the south on the front of the river Mius. Lacking any significant reserve forces, those still involved in the offensive had to be called upon to counter the Russian operations. On 10 July the Allies

BELOW Two crewmen from a Herman Goering StuG III F/8 are servicing the assault gun while under cover in an olive grove.

had landed in Sicily, thereby opening up a new front on the mainland of continental Europe. Hitler gave orders for the despatch of the II SS Panzer Corps to Italy to bolster Mussolini's regime. For the first time in the war the Germans now had to properly face fighting on two fronts, albeit after the landings at Salerno to the south of Naples had seen a further Allied incursion on Italy's mainland.

The undeniable fact was that the Russian victory in the Battle of Kursk had seen the strategic initiative on the Eastern Front pass irrevocably to the Soviet Union. Apart from localised tactical victories, the German Army was now fighting a defensive war. A whole series of counter-offensives and thereafter full-scale offensive operations by the Red Army, post-Kursk, saw the Germans thrown out of eastern Ukraine and pushed back behind the river Dnieper by the end of the year. Two months after Kursk, German panzer strength had shrunk to just 484 operational tanks, and for the first time the numbers of operational StuGs was greater. Some 524 assault guns were documented as being operational. By the year's end, the total number of assault guns across the whole of the Eastern Front in December was recorded as being 393 operational, with a further 539 in repair. There were just 21 StuHs operational, with a further 37 in repair.

The only assault gun Abteilung in Sicily on 10 July was two Batterien of StuGAbt 242 with the third having been lost in Tunisia. The arrival of nine Sturmhaubitze raised the strength of the Abteilung to 31 machines. An attempt to raise a new unit (StuGAbt 907) proved problematic due to the condition of those machines that

ABOVE **Even after the failure of Kursk, StuG units were employed almost constantly in fighting against the Red Army. Having won the strategic initiative from the Germans, the Soviet Union began its massive push towards the West, forcing the by now weakened German armies into a retreat that would not end until May 1945.**

were available. This new formation only entered combat in December 1943 with just 14 StuGs on strength. In early 1944, the newly created StuGAbt 914 arrived in Italy. It was equipped with StuGs as well as a number of Italian equivalents. The numbers of StuGs committed to the Italian theatre between 1943 and 1945 was never high.

Between 30 August and 22 September 1943, the Commander of the Sturmgeschütz Training and Replacement Battalion made an inspection tour of twelve assault gun battalions across the breadth of the Eastern Front. His post-visit report, though necessarily speaking up the value of the assault gun, nevertheless made some very interesting points.

While commenting on the improvement of the anti-tank artillery of the Russians and that they were skilfully used and feared by StuG crews, the Russian use of mines and large numbers of anti-tank rifles was also commented upon. The latter was described as an 'unpleasant' means of defence against the StuG, with even the cupola of the assault gun proving vulnerable. Captured Russian documents and prisoner interrogation had elicited the information that Soviet tank crews had been forbidden to engage in combat with Sturmgeschütz units. He quoted a

CHANGES IN ORGANISATION

Since 1941 the Sturmartillerie had witnessed more changes to its organisational structure. November had seen the issue of **K.St.N. 446**, which raised the total of StuGs in each Abteilung to 31 vehicles. All StuG units constituted since the beginning of 1943 had been authorised to field 3 Batterien each with 10 Sturmgeschütz and 1 StuG for the Stab. Thus the theoretical strength of all post-1943 established Sturmartillerie units was 31 machines, 'and every newly created Abteilung was in possession of their full complement before being sent into action'.

K.St.N. 446a – dated 1 November 1942 mandated the removal of the SdKfz 250/6 half-track ammunition carriers and their replacement by two 3-ton trucks in each StuG platoon. A new communiqué dated 1 February 1944, and given the classification **K.St.N.416b**, permitted a further StuG to be added to the Stabs (HQ) and Stabsbatterie section of both assault gun and assault howitzer Abteilungen. This was grafted on to the pre-existing **K.St.N.446** and **446a** that still obtained. What it meant was that in practice Sturmgeschütz–Abteilungen could be found deploying either 22, 31 or 45 StuGs, depending under which table of organisation they had been created or operated. There was thus no uniform size to an Abteilung. Apart from tinkering with the Abteilung structure, as in the case of the instruction described at the beginning of this section, the next major change envisaged by the OKH was to equip all Sturmgeschütz-Abteilung with 45 StuGs, albeit only four of these new 'Brigades' had been authorised and so equipped by the end of the war. These were:

1) Sturmgeschütz–Brigade 259
    May 1944 (served on the Eastern Front)
2) Sturmgeschütz–Brigade 341
    May 1944 (served in the West)
3) Sturmgeschütz–Brigade 278
    November 1944 (served on the Eastern Front)
4) Sturmgeschütz–Brigade 303
    December 1944 (served on the Eastern Front).

high-placed German commander who was heard to say that: '. . . I would rather have one Sturmgeschütz-Abteilung than an entire Panzer Division. A Regimental Commander stated that: "I prefer two Sturmgeschütz to ten Panzerkampfwagen."'

He went on to opine that:

'The Sturmgeschütz has very likely become the most valued weapon this summer. Every infantry commander speaks with enthusiasm about and recognises the capabilities of the Sturmartillerie. Aside from defending against enemy infantry assaults, the Sturmartillerie can claim a large portion of the high number of enemy tanks destroyed. The number of enemy tanks claimed in August 1943 by 11 Sturmgeschütz-Abteilungen was 423 to their own losses of 18 StuGs that are beyond repair.'

It was noted, however, that because StuG-Abteilungen were still held at Heerestruppen level, it remained their lot to be moved from one sector to another according to need. In the case of one Abteilung, it found itself operating with 11 different divisions over a period of just 10 days, while another was operating with 4 different armies over a period of 4 weeks.

One senior officer spoken to had likened this use of the Sturmartillerie as 'calling the fire brigade'. And this constant movement to and fro inevitably impacted on the serviceability of the StuGs concerned. While the vehicle had a good reputation on that score, it was noted that this constant shifting of sectors led to more 'losses from mechanical failure caused by overuse than enemy fire'. Certainly, in the period after Kursk StuG formations were in almost constant operation, with a compounding of this problem.

In November 1943 the Alkett factory at Berlin-Borgiswalde was so heavily bombed it was nearly eliminated as a production centre, in consequence of which output plummeted in December. In November, 145 StuGs had been produced up until the time of the raid; in December, because of the damage, it was only possible to assemble 24 StuGs. While alternative sites were employed – for example, chassis production for the StuG was shifted to a site in Berlin-Falkensee, with production of the StuG superstructures and final assembly relocated to Alkett's Berlin-Spandau site. However, so important was StuG production

BELOW A broken-down heavily loaded StuG III is seen under tow by another vehicle out of shot. The tarpaulin covering the fighting compartment is an attempt to prevent the ingress of dust that already covers the three crew who can be seen. In addition to the inevitable bucket, the StuG is carrying boxes with supplies and spare fuel cans. It could be that the image is from Russia in late summer 1943.

RIGHT A feature that was seen far more often as the StuG crews found themselves contending with new and effective T-34/85s, IS-IIs and heavy Russian SP guns, was the use of concrete to cover the frontal arc of the fighting compartment to lessen its vulnerability. Officialdom decried this use of the material, claiming it did not add to the defensive facilities of the StuG. Clearly, the crews disagreed – and as can be seen on the StuG III in Chapter 6 Walk-around, even those supplied to the Finns ended up with concrete applied to their hulls.

that this diminution of output could not be borne. Therefore the Krupp-Grusonwerk, which was one of the major producers of the Panzer IV, was ordered to halt production of this tank and instead rapidly adapt and start producing the Sturmgeschütz IV in December 1943.

Alkett was bombed yet again in January 1944 and MIAG in February. Even so, OKH was confident that the production target for the Sturmgeschütz would be met with Alkett producing 250 StuG IIIs, MIAG 120 and 90 StuG IV from Krupp-Grusonwerk. Even so, demand for the StuG – be it the III or the IV – always outstripped demand, so it was at this time the idea of employing the chassis of still extant Panzer III tanks was taken up again. Mk IIIs used in training units in the Ersatzheer (the Training Army) were requisitioned and Panzer IVs that had been returned to Krupp for repair and rebuilding were instead hived off for conversion to StuG IVs. These were sent to the Ersatzheer to replace their 'lost' Panzer IIIs. By the end of July 1944 this method had accounted for an extra 173 Sturmgeschütz. Nevertheless, as the subject of this text is the Sturmgeschütz III, we will not spend time addressing the StuG IV and what needs to be said will be in the context of an associated text box (right).

Not only had 1943 seen a major upsurge in the production of the Sturmgeschütz III, but the diversion of this ostensibly infantry-support weapon to other units had also prompted the General of Artillery on the General Staff to compile a document detailing the percentage allocation of newly built machines as of 23 December 1943. Whether or not this was carried out from frustration, it certainly

THE STURMGESCHÜTZ IV

The suggestion that the lost production of the StuG III arising from the bombing of the Alkett factory could be made up by adapting the Panzer IV to take the superstructure of the assault gun with its same main armament, was taken up by Hitler with alacrity. Indeed, the first example was displayed to him as early as 16 December 1943. The firm of Krupp-Gruson AG of Magdeburg that had hitherto built the Panzer IV was instructed to end the manufacture of the tank and instead employ its chassis to produce the Sturmgeschütz IV. The first 30 StuG IVs utilised the Panzer IV chassis constructed by Nibelungenwerke from their normal tank production, thus giving Krupp time to change its production line. The first Krupp-built StuG IV emerged in January 1944. The most notable change was that the driver's position was moved from within the StuG fighting compartment into an armoured cab that projected forward. It had the same engine as the StuG III – the Maybach HL120 TRM and TRM 112 – and weighed approximately the same at 23 tons. The StuG IV also adopted the same *Saukopf* mantlet used by Alkett on its StuG III and StuH. The StuG IV was the recipient of the same updates fitted to the StuG III, viz. the remote control machine gun and the *Nähverteidigungsgerät* (or close-defence weapon) mounted in the fighting compartment roof. The StuG IV was also equipped with *Schürzen*. Although the bomb damage at Alkett and MIAG was repaired and StuG production revived to the previous output, the manufacture of the StuG IV was maintained to war's end by which time 1,141 had been produced.

In assessing StuG numbers, the StuG III and IV were subsumed in the same column, no distinction being made between the two types. The StuG IV found its way into the same units as did the StuG III, being used as a support weapon and tank destroyer.

RIGHT These two excellent pictures show two crewmen inside a StuG III Ausf G in 1944. The first is of the gun-aimer. The StuG benefitted from superior sights to those employed in panzers and thus permitted this young soldier to gain a good sighting on his intended target. Trained as an artilleryman, he would 'walk' his shots on to the target and hit it by the third shot. Slightly to his rear and to his right is the cupola with the base of the scissors sight used by the StuG commander. The scissors telescope gave the commander a 10:1 magnification when compared to those of the panzers, which were 2.5:1.

exemplified the manner in which the StuG had become a necessary 'Jack of all trades' both in and outside the Wehrmacht. Just two years before, at the end of 1941, all StuGs leaving Alkett's factory were destined solely for assault gun battalions, whereas at the end of 1943 just 54% of new production was going to furnish that arm. Of the remainder, 25.3% were going

to the panzer divisions, 5.5% to the Panzerjäger units of infantry divisions, 2.2% to the Luftwaffe field divisions and 13% for service with the ever growing Waffen SS. It was without question that, for the Wehrmacht, the assault gun had become the essential weapon.

General of Artillery Lindemann, who compiled the report referenced above, acknowledged

RIGHT The loader, who was stationed on the right of the fighting compartment, proceeds to load the 75mm gun breech with a shell. Although there was an 'official' ammunition load mandated for the StuG, crews in the main modified or got rid off the fitted ammunition racks to increase the number of shells they took into combat.

In September 1943 the two companies producing the StuG were ordered to cover the main body of the StuGs leaving their factories with an anti-magnetic mine paste. A concern that the Russians and the Western Allies were going to deploy magnetic mines to place on the hulls of German AFVs saw the creation of a paste called *Zimmerit*. When hardened, this paste would neutralise the hull and thus not provide a magnetic purchase for these mines. This StuG carries the lined type of *Zimmerit* used by MIAG – the hatched pattern was scribed into the paste while it was still drying. Alkett used a waffle design, close-ups of which can be seen on the StuG in Chapter 6 Walk-around.

A close-up of the metal skirts (*Schürzen*) carried by a StuG of StuGAbt 189. One of the problems encountered, especially when operating in close country such as Italy and Normandy, was that the skirts were easily pulled off by bushes and branches. It is also worthy of note that this StuG carries a large concrete layer protecting the cupola and the top part of the fighting compartment.

that in the face of increasing panzer losses and the inability of production to compensate he:
'. . . recognised absolutely that the emergency solution of allowing substantial elements of assault gun production to be absorbed into the tank forces cannot be reversed at the moment as otherwise the tank arm would be partially lying idle. In the long term, however, it is not a satisfying situation for a weapon system to be deployed in operations for which technically it was not originally designed.'

The year 1944 would see all of the differing units employing the assault gun stretched almost to the point of exhaustion as the tempo of operations by the Red Army increased in both scale and scope from June onwards. The success of the Allied landings in Normandy in June saw the Wehrmacht truly faced with a war on two fronts.

ABOVE These three Alkett StuG III Ausf Gs were built after September 1943 because they wear the waffle-type *Zimmerit* applied by that company. They are seen advancing through a Russian village in early spring 1944. The first two StuGs carry large boxes across their engine decks.

RIGHT Repainting a StuG would normally take place when the vehicle needed to go for an overhaul or repair at the Werkstatt unit. Here, the soldier is using the standard spray gun to apply new camouflage to the StuG before it is returned to its parent unit.

ABOVE A useful photograph that shows how the *Schürzen* were hung from their attached carrying brackets on the side of this StuH. The crew is taking the opportunity to effect some basic repairs. Of note is the roughly applied *Zimmerit*. Some StuGs had this paste applied in the field.

LEFT StuG IIIs designated as a command (Befehl) assault gun mounted a Sternantenna in a ceramic housing on the right corner of the rear of the fighting compartment. This particular StuG lacks any fittings to carry *Schürzen.* The StuG is finished in an overall sand yellow with a light green overspray. It is seen in early spring 1943.

Chapter Eight

StuG III in combat 1944–45

By mid-1944 the Sturmartillerie had generated in the region of 20,000 Soviet tank kills, even though the introduction of new armour on Russian tanks and self-propelled guns was making the task of the StuG more difficult. It was beginning to show its age, but nonetheless its high output allied to its excellent optics and effective crew training saw the StuG remain in production and service through to the war's end.

OPPOSITE A major facility some miles behind the front lines acts as a collection and repair point for damaged StuGs, evidencing various degrees of rehabilitation. On the right of the picture a 1.5-tonne crane is in use while all over the site StuGs are in differing states of repair. These repair centres would be where spare parts could be sent as individual units were not permitted to order spares themselves. Some damaged machines would be returned to Germany for rebuilding, but where it was determined a machine was too far gone it would be scrapped in situ for its spares. Most of the StuGs on this site – the maintenance station of StuGAbt 210 – are mainly F/8s.

RIGHT Throughout the winter of 1943/44 the Red Army embarked on a series of offensives in the East that never gave any respite to the retreating Germans. StuG units were in continual combat even as losses began to climb.

1944 – continued expansion

Until the end of 1943 the Sturmgeschütz III had served primarily, albeit not exclusively, on the Eastern Front. The New Year would start to see this change. On 3 November 1943 Hitler penned Führer Directive No 51 (the very last of his numbered War Directives) in which he spelt out his rationale for the priorities in the following year. His main point being that it would be necessary to reinforce German forces in the West in preparation for an Allied invasion. He expressed it thus: 'I can therefore no longer take responsibility for further weakening of the West, in favour of other theatres of war. I have therefore decided to reinforce its defences.'

In practice this turned out not to be the case. The Red Army continued to exert extreme pressure across the whole front in the East and rehabilitating units in France still found themselves being transferred to that theatre in an attempt to bolster the Ostheer as it tried to contain the Russian offensive flood. Notwithstanding the large number of StuGs being produced, it was still not enough to cover the losses. Very many in the East had to be abandoned as the German Army retreated westward.

An assessment of Sturmgeschütz availability as of 1 January 1944 noted that on the Eastern Front, spread among the respective Army Groups, there was a total of 38 StuG Abteilungen deployed with a total of 1,254 assault guns. There was, however, a shortfall

RIGHT The crew of a heavily loaded StuG in the depths of the Russian winter is being asked for a tow by the driver and passengers (who are not so appropriately dressed for the cold weather) of a s.gl.Pkw Steyr Typ 1500A/01 staff car that has slid into a ditch and cannot get itself out. The StuG has *Winterketten* and also carries quite a few spares as the extensions were inclined to break off.

of 535 assault guns, and while production at Alkett and MIAG was running at a high level it could not be increased with either manufacturer to cover this number. Although these figures primarily concerned the StuG III with the StuK L/48, the overall total also embraced the StuH. These formations continued to be retained under the auspices of the Heerestruppen. These numbers excluded those StuGs and StuH that were employed by the Waffen SS divisions, Luftwaffe field units and those serving in Panzer Grenadier Divisions of which it was noted there were another 673 on strength. Although the numbers looked impressive, the reality was that due to losses and the number of vehicles under repair, 'barely one-third' of the StuG brigades were operational.

The report also embraced those Sturmgeschütz serving in the West under the auspices of High Command West. This body registered that there were 609 StuG and StuH in service there. This figure would not substantially increase before the Allied landings on 6 June 1944. The Ost Front would continue to be the main recipient of assault gun reinforcements, notwithstanding the new demands made on the numbers being produced after June 1944.

It was becoming increasingly difficult to recover 'broken-down' or 'knocked-out' StuGs, either in the face of enemy fire or because of the need to retreat. Although the report now quoted dated from 12 May 1944, it reflects what was symptomatic across the board

ABOVE A heavily laden, *Schürzen* bedecked StuH 42, with some of the skirts still evidencing their sand colour, moves across a frozen Russian landscape in the late winter of 1943/44.

LEFT With spring coming, the crew begin the process of 'de-winterising' their charge. The rear deck of this StuG IIIG is home to a very large collection of items.

ABOVE This sand-yellow Sturmhaubitze was part of the relief force that freed German forces surrounded by the Russians at Kovel in the early spring of 1944. It is still cold enough that the infantry of Panzer Grenadier Regiment 434 are still wearing their reversible winter parkas.

BELOW A MIAG-built Befehls-Sturmgeschütz in the spring of 1944. By this date all Alkett StuGs were fitted with the *Saukopf* mantlet. It is passing a captured Russian Lend-Lease-supplied Studebaker truck. Note the *Sternantenna* (star antenna) that marks out this StuG as a command vehicle. Extra tracks links are carried to provide additional protection, with the spare wheels placed for the same purpose.

for StuG units fighting in the East from the beginning of the year:

'StuG Brigade 259:
Losses in March: 7 guns through enemy fire. 34 guns destroyed, ie blown up, because of no possibility of repair or towing away.

'StuG Brigade 286:
31 guns lost in the retreat, of which 7 through enemy fire, remainder stuck in mud and through lack of towing equipment . . . 10 of the 24 left behind because of drive train damage.'

Until the spring of 1944 there is no question that the panzers and StuGs in the East had been aided by the fact that, aside from those Panzer III medium tanks still operating in that theatre (some of those returned damaged to Germany for repair were converted to StuGs), the primary armament of all others was the 75mm L/48 gun. This was, by that date, deemed to be the minimum calibre necessary to combat Soviet tanks and, indeed, equipped the bulk of German AFVs fighting in the East. This, of course, excludes panzers like the Tiger I and Panzerjäger that mounted the 88mm L/71 main gun, such as the *Nashorn*. And as long as the Soviets continued to field the T-37/76 they

RIGHT A StuG III that has just made its way through thick mud advances on a target with the commander and loader being guided by the soldier on the engine deck.

were, from point of event of the effectiveness of their main armament relative to those carried by their German opponents, obsolescent. However, by the spring of 1944, the steps taken by the Red Army in the months after Kursk to rectify this reality began to manifest itself with the emergence on to the battlefields of the East, a whole tranche of new machines. The T-34, the mainstay of the Red Army tank arm, was upgraded with a new three-man turret mounting an 85mm main gun and a cupola as standard, giving the tank commander a far better 'situational awareness'. It was also the case that the quality of these new T-34s was better. Although this 'new' T-34 did not negate the technical superiority of the Panther and Tiger I, it was more effective than the most numerous panzer, the Mk IV. When allied to the immensity of its production when compared to that of the Germans, the introduction of the T-34/85 was to provide a real problem for the German Army. Nor was it alone, for other new machines were emerging that also served to swing the armour balance in the Red Army's favour. Spring 1944 also saw the emergence of the new IS-2 heavy tank armed with a 122mm main gun. These began to equip the heavy tank regiments, with each fielding 21 tanks. They would really make an impact in Operation 'Bagration' in late June 1944.

CENTRE This photograph enables us to view the *Saukopf* mantlet fitted by Alkett to its StuGs from October 1943. This vehicle is without *Zimmerit* so its production date is difficult to place. The finish of the StuG is *Sandgelb* (sand yellow) the standard base colour used on German AFVs since February 1943.

RIGHT The whole of the engine deck of this StuG is being raised with the help of a crane lorry. The *Zimmerit* is the waffle design denoting that the vehicle was built by Alkett. With the deck off the Werkstatt crew can begin to work on the engine.

155

There were also the Soviet assault guns. The first attempt to produce such a type had led to the less than successful SU-122, but it was replaced in the autumn of 1943 by the SU-85, being equipped with the same gun as the updated T-34. In 1944, this was in turn replaced by the SU-100, whose main gun was effective against nearly all German armour. The year 1944 would also see the emergence of heavier self-propelled guns such as the ISU-122 and ISU-152. Whereas at the beginning of 1944, self-propelled guns numbered 3,300 in the Red Army, by the year's end expanding production of the types would see the total rise to over 10,000. This equated to some 29% of the Red Army inventory. For the first time the StuG Abteilungen in the East were being faced with quantity allied to quality and it was evident, as the year progressed, that the StuG, even armed with the 75mm StuK L/48, was no longer the battlefield force it had been the previous year. The need for its replacement was becoming apparent. This was succinctly expressed in a report of 16 February 1944:

'Army Group South reports that in most recent combats, Soviet assault guns appeared which, as KV-14 and 85, have 140mm frontal armour. This creates the problem of which artillery calibre will be able to defeat such armour. Even up to calibre length 71, the effectiveness of 75mm round is inadequate. It must be investigated whether at short notice the 88mm calibre must be adopted by the assault artillery.'

It was also recognised that: 'At long range (over 2,000m) the heavy Soviet tanks and assault guns are superior in terms of both calibre and effectiveness.'

In principle, the Jagdpanzer IV (JgPz IV, and then the JgPz IV/70 – the latter mounting the same gun as that on the Panther) was envisaged as supplanting, then replacing the StuG III. In reality, the war situation was such that notwithstanding the growing limitations of the StuG, these had to be lived with as it was necessary to maintain the high level of production and employment. By mid-1944, the assault artillery based on the StuG III and StuH

would be limited to a maximum of 45 brigades, although it was agreed in principle that the number of vehicles per brigade could be raised to 45. This was to be achieved by increasing the number of StuGs allocated to the assault artillery and especially of the proportion of StuH.

On 8 June 1944, the official national newspaper of Germany and of the Nazi Party, the *Volkischer Beobachter*, carried a propagandist article that lauded the performance of the Sturmartillerie units of the Wehrmacht in their battles with the armoured formations of the Red Army on the Eastern Front. Although by this date the assault gun was serving in formations other than just those of the artillery – for it had perforce also found its way into tank divisions and Panzerjäger units – it was still the case that the bulk of these machines were being operated by the artillery arm in their many assault gun Abteilungen/Brigaden. The headline read:

'Artillery destroyed 20,000 tanks in Eastern Campaign.

'For months our infantry has been engaged in a costly battle against the Soviet masses

ABOVE The Jagdpanzer IV was designed by Krupp utilising the hull, transmission and running gear of the Panzer IV to which a new superstructure was added with sloped welded armour. Originally intended to carry the 75mm L/70 main gun – the same as that carried on the Panther – the shortage of this weapon saw the 75mm L/48 used instead. Conceptually, it was understood by many to be a more effective StuG.

BELOW When in 1944 the L/70 gun did become available this was fitted, the end result being the 75mm Jagdpanzer IV/70. Over 1,500 Jagdpanzer IVs and 300 IV/70s were built by 1945.

BELOW A StuG with very crudely applied concrete supplementary armour. Built by Alkett and still retaining its *Zimmerit* coating, it is pictured in the late summer or early autumn of 1944. Note the steel return rollers, introduced in November 1943.

and their tanks. As their most faithful helper in this desperate struggle against a powerful opponent, the artillery stands side by side as trusted comrades in arms with the infantry. The assault guns of the artillery have achieved major successes in this untiring battle against the tanks. Since the beginning of the Eastern Campaign they have destroyed 15,000 enemy

tanks. This figure not only emphasises the ferocity of the fighting and the quality of German arms, but also proves the particular significance of the as yet young assault artillery in their defensive battles against Bolshevism.'

This impression of the sheer mass of the Soviet war matériél becomes even clearer when one bears in mind that additionally the Army

and divisional artillery – whose primary task is in other sectors – as bastions of the defensive battle, have neutralised a further 5,000 tanks, so that since the beginning of the Eastern Campaign alone, the artillery has destroyed 20,000 tanks.

The StuG in the Normandy Campaign

Two days before the publication of that article, British, American and Canadian forces had landed on the beaches of Normandy. Here is not the place to discuss the conduct of the Normandy Campaign, but to examine the role of the StuG formations in the two months of battles wherein the Germans tried desperately to contain the Allies from breaking out of their lodgement, during which some 453 StuG IIIs, StuHs and StuG IVs were employed in the fighting.

Just three StuG Brigaden were employed in Normandy – namely the 341st, 394th and 902nd. Also committed was the Luftwaffe Fallschirm-Sturmgeschütz Brigade. All except the 341st had 45 StuGs on strength, while the others were fielding 31 vehicles. The three Army

Brigaden were at full strength when they arrived in Normandy and it is assumed that this was also the case with the Luftwaffe unit.

Six of the infantry divisions in the theatre were fielding a Panzerjäger Abteilung, of which one company was comprised of StuGs, with these having ten StuGs each. The Waffen SS panzer divisions were also deploying StuGs in lieu of proper tank destroyers in their Panzerjäger Abteilungen with even their premiere formations, namely the 1st and 2nd Panzer Divisions, deploying 45 StuGs in each. But in the case of the latterly formed 9th and 10th SS Panzer Divisions, the title was really a misnomer, as neither possessed a Panzer-Abteilung, with two of the panzer companies being substituted with StuGs. The 9th SS-Panzer Division 'Hohenstaufen' fielded 40 StuGs and the 10th SS Panzer Division 'Frundsberg' two less. The 17th SS Panzer-Grenadier Division 'Gotz von Berlichingen' had a StuG III battalion with 42 on strength at the time of its deployment to Normandy.

There were other StuGs serving in a number of Army formations such as the 9th Panzer Division that had 6 StuGs on strength and 2 Funklenk units – notably 4/Panzer Abteilung

LEFT There are few pictures of StuGs in Normandy. Indeed, this Befehls-Sturmgeschütz was caught by the photographer just before 6 June 1944. It mounts the side-rails for the *Schürzen*, wears *Zimmerit* and is in very good condition. It is clearly, at the time, a relatively new-build machine, although without seeing the mantlet it is not possible to say whether it was built by Alkett or MIAG. Very few of the quite large number of StuGs that served in Normandy survived the campaign. Until the end of the war, far fewer assault guns served in the West when compared to the still large numbers serving on the Eastern Front.

RIGHT An American
soldier examines a
burned-out StuG III in
Normandy.

301 (Fkl) with 6 and the Panzer-Kompanie 316
(Fkl) with 10.

It is not possible to say with certainty
how many StuGs were sent to Normandy
as replacements as it seems no one source
detailed such. One list shows 17 StuG IIIs and
10 StuG IVs being sent to the 'West' at the end
of July. It is also the case that the ratio of StuH
to StuGs serving Normandy is not known. Of
the 10 panzer units that reported their losses
between D-Day and 8 July, it was noted that 25
StuGs had been 'written-off' in the fighting.

Guderian, in his capacity as Inspector
General of Panzer Troops, sent Hitler a
detailed report on German tank performance
in Normandy at the end of June, in the course
of which he made the following observations
about the Sturmgeschütz. (The rider to this is
that Guderian was at the time trying to stop
Hitler ordering that all Panzer IV production be
converted to Sturmgeschütz production.)

*'Experience reports from Sicily, Italy and
Normandy comparing the Panzer IV to the
Sturmgeschütz unanimously state that when
employed on coastal roads, in mountainous
terrain, and in the sunken lanes and hedges
of Normandy, the Sturmgeschütz is both
tactically and technically considerably less
favoured than the PzKpfw IV. The terrain
makes impossible, or at least severely limits
aiming the Sturmgeschütz to the sides.*

*'Based on the lastest observations
reported by General Thomale in Paris and
reports from the Panzer-Offizier Ob.West,
employment
of the Sturmgeschütz in the sunken lanes
and the hedges of Normandy is difficult
because the gun is mounted too low. In
contrast the Panzerkampfwagen can fire
out of the sunken lanes and also over the
hedges because of the height of the gun and
traversable turret.'*

The StuG units fought at their most effective
when they were deployed to operate in fixed
positions and could be well camouflaged. The
main gun of the StuG was fully able to deal
with the main British and US tanks employed
in Normandy such as the M4 and the British
Cromwell. The heavily armoured Churchill in its
latest incarnation was a more difficult adversary,
but if ambushed could still be dealt with.
German accounts of StuG operations in the
theatre are not great, but a short consideration
of the fate of StuG-Brigade 341 can convey
some sense of the nature of the combat in
Normandy.

Although this unit was formed in May 1943 and from November was deployed to France to work up and was 'in-country' when the invasion took place, StuG-Brigade 341 was not deployed to Normandy until 27 July, when it was thrown into the effort to prevent the American advance after the launch of Operation 'Cobra' two days before. Committed in the Avranches area, the brigade was involved in heavy fighting with US armoured forces and by 1 August the 1st Batterie lost 12 of its 14 StuGs. This was followed soon thereafter by the other two Batterien also losing theirs. Although reinforcements were sent, it lost all of its StuGs for the second time, in consequence mainly because of the efficacy of Allied air power. Re-equipped for the third time, the brigade survived the campaign but was sufficiently devastated once again, pulled back to Germany and rebuilt for the third time.

Most of the StuGs deployed to Normandy were either destroyed or lost when the Falaise Pocket was closed.

In the general report on the state of the Sturmartillerie at the beginning of September 1944, just three brigades – the 341st, 394th and 902nd – were listed as being operational, and these could only muster a paltry 18 serviceable StuGs between them. A major and very rapid reinforcement programme began to re-equip these Brigaden.

Catastrophe in the East

Three weeks after D-Day the Red Army launched one of its largest ever offensives on 22 June – the third anniversary of the German invasion – directed at the destruction of Army Group Centre. What followed was the greatest defeat in German military history. Even before the offensive began there were only two panzer units – the 20 Pz.Div and s.Pz.Abt 501 – fielding the pathetically small number of just 85 operational tanks – and 404 StuGs. In the days following 28 out of the 38 German divisions were swept from the Order of Battle – routed and destroyed. The bulk of the number of German tanks and assault guns was submerged by a tidal wave of Soviet armour, swept away by the huge numbers of T-34/85 medium tanks and large numbers of the IS-II heavy tank. By the time 'Bagration' was over the remnants of the German formations had been pushed back into East Prussia.

As of 1 September 1944, an assessment in the Sturmartillerie situation in the East revealed that there was a shortage of 247 StuGs, and

ABOVE A StuG III is among the casualties of Allied air attacks around Falaise.

RIGHT An ornately camouflaged late-build StuH is seen here advancing across snow-covered fields in East Prussia or Poland in the winter of 1944/45. It has the large *Saukopf* mantlet to house the 105mm howitzer.

BELOW Beginning in September 1944, Alkett stopped fitting the 105mm howitzer on their StuHs with a muzzle brake. The addition of a reinforced barrel mechanism also required Alkett to refit the box-type bolted mantlet. This was standard on the StuH through to the end of the war.

of those listed as being available, just 534 were operational. However, outside these artillery Brigaden there were another 1,629 StuGs deployed. In toto, on both the Eastern and Western Fronts, the Army had a total of 2,734 StuGs and StuHs on strength. However, these figures do not take account of the catastrophe that was now visited on the StuG units serving with Army Group South in Ukraine as the Soviet offensive into Rumania tore into the Sturmgeschütz strength on that Front. In

the autumn, the General of Artillery listed the total number of assault gun losses between January and August 1944 on all Fronts to have been 2,928, with there being a shortfall of 678 machines as of 1 September 1944.

After the close of 'Bagration' the Soviet offensive focus shifted back to the south and in August, with the Red Army offensive into Rumania, there were 9 intact assault gun Brigaden on strength. Army Headquarters (AOK) listed 6. These were Brigade Nos: 236,

A StuH in the late war 'ambush' camouflage scheme operating in Hungary in late 1944. Note that it carries a remotely controlled machine gun on the roof in the front of the loader's hatch. It is also lacking a muzzle brake, dating the production of this machine to after September 1944 and probably dating the picture to the later autumn of that year.

RIGHT An Alkett-built StuG wearing thickly applied concrete armour and waffle Zimmerit.

239, 243, 278, 286 and 911; and in AOK 8: just 228, 325 and 905. With exception of just three that managed to survive in a pitiful state the other brigades were destroyed. That meant that of the total of 270 operational at the beginning of the Soviet offensive, just 38 survived.

The year 1944 was the peak year of Sturmgeschütz production, with 3,850 StuG IIIs with L/48, 903 Sturmhaubitze and 1,006 Sturmgeschütz IVs leaving the assembly lines despite air raids. MIAG suffered 6 raids throughout 1944, with Krupp-Gruson in Magdeburg experiencing 5. Even then output for these two factories remained high, resulting in the fairly even replacement of machines, except in the second half of the year when losses at the Front became very high. Nonetheless,

BELOW An abandoned StuG beside a road in the Ardennes during the Battle of the Bulge.

by Christmas 1944 the Army had 48 StuG Brigaden on strength – that is 3 more than the mandated total of 45. Thus the Sturmartillerie had continued to expand up until 1944.

The Sturmartillerie was involved in the last major German offensive of the war – Operation 'Watch on the Rhine', better known as the Battle of the Bulge. Although the operation was a total failure strategically, on a tactical level the Sturmartillerie continued to prove its effectiveness in German eyes. Not the least reason being that unlike in the East where the Red Army was fielding superior equipment, in the West (and that included in the Ardennes) the assault gun still found itself able to deal effectively with most Allied armour, although the use of the M4A3E2 'Jumbo' Sherman proved invulnerable to the 75mm L/48 even at short ranges. The following is part of a report of an artillery Oberstleutnant, of his experiences in the Ardennes offensive. Of the performance of the Sturmartillerie he had this to say:

'. . . the Sturmartillerie had proven its value also in the West [having done so in the East] where it is the backbone of our infantry. Combat losses in personnel and material are high. . . . Night attacks have proven most effective. Sturmgeschütz were the first to enter St Vith at night. The enemy, who until then put up a dogged defence, gave up the struggle for the city and retreated. In Krombach, southwest of St Vith, seven Sturmgeschütz succeeded in taking the city, which was defended by 30 tanks, in a night attack. The enemy lost 15 tanks, many of which were lightly damaged. Both attacks were carried out in bright moonlight.'

The following table shows numbers and categories for the StuG in the theatres of war. The first figure shows the numbers as of the end of January 1945 with the second (after the /) indicating numbers as of 14 April. Note there are no figures for those machines under delivery for that date.

Theatre	Operational	Under repair	Under delivery	Total
Eastern armies	1,803/515	394/110		2,197/625
Denmark and Norway	48/36	4/3		52/39
Western Europe	340/29	376/16		716/45
Italy	265/109	80/14		345/123
Balkans	17/18	8/0		25/18
Total	2,473/707	862/143		3,335/850

Thereafter, the end for Germany was measured in weeks as the vice closed around the Reich from both East and West. In these battles the assault gun was encountered, albeit in declining numbers. Even though 863 StuG IIIs and 80 StuHs were manufactured by Alkett

RIGHT The city of Kolberg in Pomerania was taken by the Russians in March 1945 after a ferocious battle. The image here is of an early StuG refitted with a 75mm StuK L/48 main gun and given a very extensive covering of concrete on the roof of the fighting compartment. Also of interest is the extended cover over the driver's visor which, elsewhere in this text, is suggested as being something fitted by the Finns alone.

LEFT This second photograph from Kolberg shows a similar retrofitted 75mm L/48 main gun on a StuG III Ausf D. Few photographs have turned up since the war to suggest that this was a common occurrence and indeed it may have been carried out only by a Werkstatt in Kolberg itself.

OPPOSITE **This late variant of a StuG III Ausf G has evidently fallen foul of a morass of mud and been abandoned by its crew. Nonetheless it allows us to focus on a number of significant details. The vehicle can be dated from after September 1944 as that is when Alkett began fitting the cast steel *Saukopf* mantlet with an aperture for a coaxial machine gun. Mounted ahead of the loader's hatch it also carries the remotely controlled machine gun that was fired from within the fighting compartment. In front of that is the hatch for the close-in defence weapon.**

and MIAG between January and April, most of these were consumed in the ferocious fighting in the East as the Red Army closed in on, and finally took, Berlin, forcing the German surrender of the city on 2 May. The same fate befell those few remaining StuG units attempting to hold the Allied flood into Germany after the defeat in the Battle of the Ruhr and the crossing of the Rhine.

Finale

The combat life of the Sturmgeschütz was short – from May 1940 through to May 1945. There is no doubt that in German eyes the machine was a great success. Indeed, it could be said that without the Sturmartillerie and the employment of the StuG in other units such as panzer divisions and panzer-grenadier divisions, the German Army could not have survived for as long as it did. Notwithstanding its limitations, it truly became the 'essential machine' operated by the Wehrmacht, especially in its primary theatre of operations from 1941 through to 1945 – that of the Eastern Front. What accounts for the incredible tally of Soviet armour claimed destroyed by the Sturmartillerie by 1944? I quote my friend Thomas Anderson's succinct analysis, when he says that the reasons for the StuG's success were as follows:

'The Soviet Union was a country of vast plains (steppes) which, in many regions, were ideal for massed tank attacks. With the introduction of the Selbstfahrlafette-Zielenferrohr (Sfl-ZF) gun sight, Sturmgeschütz were able to fight enemy tanks at long range, despite

having a limited traverse. This ability remained late into the war, despite having inferior armour protection and firepower.'

He also points that the *espirit de corps* among members of the Sturmartillerie was outstanding. Training and leadership were apparently very good. And it was also the case that German tactics on the battlefield proved to be far superior, especially in the East. In a sense it could be argued that the StuG was a creature that was best employed and most successful on the vast plains of the Eastern Front.

Although the concept of a turretless AFV mounting a heavy gun in an armoured casemate was only emulated by the Red Army, who produced a series of powerfully armed assault-gun-type machines, the concept itself died with the end of the war. Although it could be argued that it was revived by the Germans with the Jagdpanzer 90 in the 1950s–60s and the Swedish Army with the S-Type tank, which had no turret and like the assault gun, turned on its tracks to aim at its target, the concept itself has found no real traction in post-war armies – the preference being for the main battle tank (MBT). This is not to say that there have been voices raised – particularly at the time of the greatest preponderance of Warsaw Pact armour over that possessed by NATO – that the idea of a modern StuG should be revisited. Ultimately it all came to nothing.

BELOW **These Sturmgeschütz IIIs were recovered from the town of Yambol near the border with Turkey in February 2008. They had been purchased by the Bulgarian Army in the Second World War. A total of 55 were delivered between February and December 1943 to equip tank destroyer units of the Bulgarian Army. During the Cold War they were stationed near the border to contest any attempt by the Turkish Army to invade Bulgaria.** (*Boryana Katsarova/AFP/Getty Images*)

Bibliography and sources

Anderson, Thomas, *History of Panzerwaffe*, Vols 1 and 2 (Osprey, 2015 and 2017)
Sturmgeschütz, Vols 1 and 2 (Osprey, 2016 and 2017)

Vorwärts Immer, Rückwärts Nimmer! (History Facts, 2010)
Barnett, Corelli, *Hitler's Generals* (Weidenfeld and Nicholson, 1995)

Chamberlain, Doyle and Jentz, *Encyclopedia of German Tanks of World War II* (Arms and Armour Press, 1978)

Healy, Mark, *Zitadelle* (The History Press, 2008)

Jaugitz, Marcus, Funklenkpanzer (J.J Fedorowicz, 2001)

Kurowski, Franz, *Sturmgeschütz Vor!* (J.J Fedorowicz, 1999)

Lefevre, Eric, *Panzers in Normandy Then and Now* (After the Battle, 1983)

McGuirl, Thomas and Spezzano, Remy, God, *Honor, Fatherland* (RZM Imports, 1997)

Müller, Peter and Zimmermann, Wolfagang, *Sturmgeschütz III*, Vols 1 and 2 (History Facts, 2009 and 2011)

Raus, Erhard, *Panzer Operations* (Da Capo, 2003)

Spielberger, Walter J., *Sturmgeschütz and its variants* (Schiffer Military, 1993)
Panzer III and its variants (Schiffer Military, 1993)

Taylor, Brian, Barbarossa to Berlin, Vols 1 and 2 (Spellmount Books, 2003 and 2005)

Zaloga, Steven J., *Armored Champion* (Stackpole Books, 2015)

Zetterling, Niklas, *Kursk 1943* (Cass, 2000)
Normandy 1944 (J.J Fedorowicz, 2000)

Index